THE PLAYS OF T.S. ELIOT

THE PLAYS OF T.S. ELIOT

Shubha Tiwari
Maneesha Tiwari

PUBLISHERS & DISTRIBUTORS (P) LTD

Published by
ATLANTIC
PUBLISHERS & DISTRIBUTORS (P) LTD

B-2, Vishal Enclave, Opp. Rajouri Garden,
New Delhi-110027
Phones : 25413460, 25429987, 25466842

Sales Office
7/22, Ansari Road, Darya Ganj,
New Delhi-110002
Phones : 23273880, 23275880, 23280451
Fax : 91-11-23285873
web : www.atlanticbooks.com
e-mail : info@atlanticbooks.com

Copyright © Atlantic Publishers and Distributors (P) Ltd., 2007

ISBN 81-269-0649-9

All rights reserved. No part of this publication may be reproduced, stored in a retrieval system, transmitted or utilized in any form or by any means, electronic, mechanical, photocopying, recording or otherwise, without the prior permission of the copyright owner. Application for such permission should be addressed to the publisher.

Printed in India
at Nice Printing Press, Delhi

Preface

In modern English drama there has been a trend to revive the age-old convention of the chorus. Several experiments have been conducted to adopt it to suit the changing conditions of time and stage. This emergence of chorus has been so conspicuous that whosoever goes through any of the modern plays, especially the poetic plays, is most likely to be struck by the novelty of their techniques and the strikingly unique position that the chorus enjoys in them.

In this tradition of poetic plays came the great modern master, T.S. Eliot, whose contribution in this field is of immense value. Eliot explored the drama of the Elizabethans and the Ancients and put into it a new sense of renaissance, wonder and greatness. His experiments with the chorus have evolved a new dramatic form. In this context Eliot's dramatic technique along with the use of the chorus in different plays has been thoroughly studied in the present research project, exploring the potential of the chorus as a powerful dramatic convention in modern drama, projecting and assessing Eliot's contribution to the field.

In the Introduction an effort has been made to analyse the nature and functions of the chorus, simultaneously tracing its origin and development from the temple of Dionysus right up to its modern adaptations in the poetic plays of the twentieth century. How initially the dithyrambic choral odes were sung into the temple of Dionysus and how gradually they developed into Greek tragic drama wherein chorus plays a very important part. It could expound the past, comment on the present and forebode the future. It provided the poet with a mouthpiece and the spectator with a counterpart of himself and thus formed a foreground of common humanity. But with the development of dramatic art, the battle of the Individual against the Group started which gradually diminished the importance of the chorus. Historically, the chorus possesses a chequered history of its development. The Humanist and the Individualistic trends accounted for the decline of the chorus in the Renaissance period and Elizabethan drama. Milton, however, tried to revive the Greek form of drama with the chorus as the central convention and his experiment was later followed by Shelley, Byron, Arnold and Swinburne. But the most significant attempts at reviving the chorus were made in modern times by the 'poets of the theatre' in their poetic plays. In this tradition T.S. Eliot, whose contribution is the main subject of the present research project, has been studied in six different chapters.

In the Second Chapter a study of his earlier fragments has been made. In *Sweeney Agonistes* he has fused the ancient and the modern together to present a powerful piece of art. Herein he has combined the music of the twentieth century with the technique of Greek drama, thus using the metaphysical technique of combining together the trivial and the serious.

Then we have *The Rock*, a pageant play, as his next excursion into drama. The ten choruses which Eliot wrote embody a spiritual message of Christian theology along with his mystic revelation of the Eternity. In these choral odes we find beautiful pieces of meditative poetry. But the episodes of the play are loosely linked together by the chorus. Despite its weaknesses, *The Rock* is an important stage in the development of Eliot's dramatic career. It prepared him for his coming masterpiece.

In the Third Chapter the role of the chorus in Eliot's masterpiece *Murder in the Cathedral* has been discussed. The Women of Canterbury provide a powerful chorus to the play. They give expression to the communal feeling which usually runs deeper than individual feeling. The choruses of *Murder in the Cathedral* are perhaps the greatest things in the play. There is nothing else like this in English. In fact we have to go back to Greek tragedy to find choral writings with which they can be best compared.

In the Fourth Chapter it has been discussed how in *The Family Reunion* Eliot has shown some rethinking in the use of the chorus. Here Eliot has tried to integrate the chorus more closely into the central design of the play. In this play chorus actually consists of Harry's Uncles and Aunts, who have also been assigned separate roles, quite different from their collective role as chorus. They are stock English types slightly caricatured. Unlike the usual Greek chorus their role is not to illuminate the action but to express their baffled inability to understand what is happening. Thus, unlike the previous play the chorus in *The Family Reunion* has a limited role to play.

In the Fifth Chapter an attempt has been made to find out why and how Eliot in *The Cocktail Party* decides to drop the formal chorus, but uses certain compensatory devices which fill the vacuum so caused and the choric function continues to be performed by some device or the other. One such device is the use of the mythical method. Through this method Eliot has been able to create a double pattern in his play so that the audience might discern one meaning at the surface level while the myth might evoke another meaning at the deeper level. Thus with all its symbolism and suggestivity the mythical method works as a latent chorus in the later plays of Eliot. Then besides discarding the formal use of the chorus, Eliot interfuses the chorus into the characters of the play by devising the special machinery of the *The Guardian*, who besides being the mouthpiece of the dramatist also guide the action of the play and make a meaningful commentary on other characters and thus performs important choric function. Thus, the chorus in this play has been introduced with a mask on.

In the Sixth Chapter an analysis of his last play *The Elder Statesman* shows how the play depicts the theme of 'guilt and expatiation' in terms of Sophocles' version of *Oedipus at Colonus*. The major symbol in the play is the mask, and the stripping off the false masks before death makes up the chief dramatic action of the play. In a way *The Elder Statesman* is a play not so much about Lord Claverton as about Everyman. It resembles a morality play both in respect of structure as well as versification. In this play there is no formal use of the chorus.

However, the Hamlet-like soliloquies of Lord Claverton project the inner permutations of the protagonist, a function which was many times allotted to the chorus. Moreover, the incorporation of the novel machinery in the form of ghosts, makes the chorus peep behind the curtain. Thus, it can be safely concluded that in the later plays of Eliot, the chorus may not be physically present on the stage, it is definitely standing in the wings.

The Seventh Chapter, a conclusion, gives the gist of the whole study, presenting the generalized inferences drawn during the course of the analysis of different plays. It also provides an assessment of the use of the chorus by Eliot in its totality, giving a complete picture of its dramatic significance.

It is hoped that students, scholars and general readers of English literature will find this book both useful and enjoyable.

We thank all those persons who rendered unstinted help and support in preparing this book.

Our special thanks go to Dr. K.R. Gupta, Chairman, Atlantic Publishers and Distributors (P) Ltd., New Delhi, for the confidence evinced in us, and also for seeing the book through the press.

SHUBHA TIWARI
MANEESHA TIWARI

Contents

Preface	*v*
1. Introduction	1
2. *Sweeney Agonistes and Other Fragments*	41
3. *Murder in the Cathedral*	80
4. *The Family Reunion*	107
5. *The Cocktail Party*	131
6. *The Elder Statesman*	152
7. Conclusion	173
Chronology	192
Bibliography	194

1 Introduction

(A) CHORUS: ITS MEANING, NATURE AND FUNCTIONS

Before analyzing the chorus as a dramatic convention, it may be natural to enquire into the meaning, nature and significance of conventions in literature, which are usually a device, principle, procedure or form generally accepted, through which there is an agreement between the writer and his readers (or audience) and which allows him various freedoms and restrictions. The term is especially relevant to drama. The stage itself, as a physical object and area, establishes a convention by creating boundaries and limitations. The division of a play into acts and scenes is a dramatic convention, as are soliloquies and asides. Flashbacks and foreshadowing are also examples of literary conventions. The audience is prepared to suspend disbelief and to experience a representation of scenery and action, of lighting and words. The use of verse, blank or rhymed, dance, song, a chorus, the unities, the aside, the soliloquy, are all examples of dramatic conventions. Working with in the conventions and using them to the best possible advantage is essential to the art of the dramatist. The people in the audience are a party to the agreement and their acceptance makes the dramatic illusion possible.

In fact every writer accepts conventions as soon as he begins to write. It can be argued that conventions are essential to all literature as necessary and convenient ways of working within the limitations of the medium of words. Periodically conventions are broken or replaced. Wordsworth's rejection of 18th century poetic diction is an obvious instance; so is the substitution, in drama, of naturalistic conventions for the traditional dramatic ones. Chorus has also been one such dramatic convention, which has passed through a chequered history through the ages.

So it may be quite pertinent to analyse the meaning, nature and functions of the Chorus and its history through the ages.

'Chorus' is derived from the Greek work *Choros* which originally meant a dance, accompanied by singing. It was initially employed at the festivals held in honour of Gods, especially of Dionysus and gradually became an essential part of the Early Greek Drama and a powerful dramatic convention. This part was at first predominant but later became subordinate to that of the actors.

Chorus also denotes "a body of singers in opera, oratorio, cantatas, etc. who sing the music written for large groups of voices in parts for each type of voice: soprano or treble, contralto or alto, tenor and bass. However, the chorus may be distinguished from a glee, which is properly written for single voices to each part. Hence when a portion of a song is to be sung, not by a single singer but by a number of singers, it is styled a *Chorus*."[1]

Originally, "the Chorus was trained by the poet himself, who was known in this capacity as *Chorodidaskalos*. The leader of the chorus was called the Coryphacus. The portions of a drama assigned to the chorus might be written partly in iambic (for dialogue) partly in anapestic measure (chiefly for entrance and exit of the chorus), but consisted mainly of lyrics. The Chorus was frequently divided into two semi-choruses, who sung alternate stanzas; but whether particular lines were sung by the whole chorus, by part of it, or by a single voice, is often, in the absence of stage directions, a matter of more or less probable conjecture."[2]

If we imagine ourselves to be in a Greek theatre we can visualize how the chorus stood at the Orchestra, in the middle of the theatre, occupying a central position, singing and dancing and delivering its lyrical odes as a part of the dramatic ritual. It addressed its odes to the actor as also to the auditor and thus provided a bridge between the two, leading to a constant interaction between the Stage and the Audience.

The audience would, in the normal course, react to the action on the stage. But all the reactions would not be worthy of communication. Very often they would take the shape of muttering or shouting and would not be worthy of survival. Still, however, they would embody a very vital part of the performance. The chorus sifted these reactions of the audience to the drama and distilled the finer parts. Thus the part played by the chorus was in that way tied up integrally with the drama proper. It served as a concentrating medium for the numerous reactions of the audience. It thus made some sort of distillation and was something of a sieve. In the modern realistic drama the reactions of the audience are left unsatisfied, while in Greek theatre and so also in many of its modern adaptations, the reactions of the audience are conveyed to the Stage through the chorus. Thus Schlegel has rightly described the chorus as 'the ideal spectator'.

On the other hand, the chorus also underlines the bearing of the drama for each individual auditor. In this role the chorus acts as the mouthpiece of the dramatist and has a powerful impact on the audience. The wisdom of the drama is underlined by the chorus and in this way the drama is universalized. While the tragic protagonists act out their defiance of the limits subscribed by the Gods for men, the chorus expresses the fears, hopes and judgment of the polity or the average citizen. In this way their judgment is the verdict of history.

Thus the chorus embodies the finer reactions of the audience at any point in drama. On the other hand it also underlines the bearing of the drama for the audience. Both ways the chorus becomes a critic of the drama. It provides a running commentary on the action, as the play moves on. Thus you have a sort of double experience in a Greek play, because "we as audience see it doubly, by seeing its effect on other people."[3]

"Dramatically, the chorus can serve many purposes. It can work as a mouthpiece of the dramatist. It can expound the past, comment on the present and illuminate the future. It provides the spectator with a counterpart of himself. It presents the inside permutations of common humanity, and has the capacity to portray human situation in its relevant perspective. With its pure poetry it can transmogrify lamentation into music; horror into peace and serious into the sublime. On the negative side the chorus was deliberately dropped by many a dramatist, since they regarded it as an encumbrance."[4]

The chorus has also been censured as an absurdity, in as much as, representing a crowd, it shows a secret transaction on the soul being carried on before the public—an objection which, of course, might be applied to the condemnation of the whole Tragic Drama, whereby the inmost agonies of contending souls are laid bare to crowded benches.

Technically, however, "the chorus was never a mere luxury. It performed specific functions. Originally, it used to impersonate a definite group of people. It existed 'in' the play, not as an impersonal voice, but as an anonymous collectively, which usually pushed it away from the center where everything happened. It was further removed from the action of the play, when it separated from the speaking actions of the orchestra, where it had room enough to dance. In this way half in and half out of the action, the chorus performed its functions, and provided an added intensity to the inner meaning of the play."[5]

The chorus is the most obvious conventional mouthpiece for the author, but there are subtle means of commentary within the action itself. A character may be depersonalized temporarily to convey a piece of information or suggest a point of view, which will orientate the reactions of the audience. In a theatre governed by conventions, the audience will make the necessary adjustment to the movement out of character quite unconsciously. Conventions are thus seen to be liberating agencies, allowing the author to supplement the action by information and insights, which will illuminate it. They are basically tacit agreements between the author and the audience that character shall behave or speak in a way which is not true to life but which will broaden the scope of the drama. Such a running commentary is often found in Shakespeare coming from one particular character. Lear's Fool is a running criticism; so is Touchstone; so is Feste. Thus Shakespeare's Fools carry on the choric function.

T.S. Eliot has also confessed to a similar use in his plays: "My intention was to have one character whose sensibility and intelligence should be on the plane of the most sensitive and intelligent members of the audience; his speeches should be addressed to them as much as to the other personages in the play or rather should be addressed to the latter, who were to be material, literal minded and visionless, with the consciousness of being overheard by the former."[6]

In a more fundamental way Greek tragedy is one single experience. The chorus should be absolutely integral to the experience. If the chorus is removed, the play should fall to pieces. Sometimes, however, the choric ode might be treated as music and dance for its own sake; this is what happened in Euripides and subsequent dramatists. This danger is always there. Hence the chorus has to be strictly integral to the play. Accordingly, speaking about the chorus, Aristotle pronounced the much needed warning: "The chorus too should be regarded as one of the actors; it should be an integral part of the whole, and share in the action that which it has in Sophocles rather than in Euripides."[7] This suggests that by Aristotle's time the chorus and the drama proper had almost come to be separated—a practice, which he condemned.

Originally the chorus was a group of performers at a religious festival, especially fertility rites. By some process of grafting or symbiosis Greek tragedy acquired (or grew out of) these choral rites. At any rate, the chorus becomes an essential and integral part of Greek tragic drama. In Greek tragedies (especially those of Aeschylus and Sophocles), chorus represented a group of people who served mainly as commentators on the characters and events. They added to the audience's understanding of the play by expressing traditional moral, religious, and social attitudes. The chorus consisted of Athenian citizens who were not professional actors. The chorus rejoiced in the triumph of the Good; it wailed aloud its grief, and sympathized with the woe of the puppets of the Gods. It entered deeply into the interest of their fortunes and misfortunes, yet it stood apart, outside of triumph and failure. It was the "Vox Humana" amid the storm and thunder of the Gods. The tragic chorus represented with wonderful truth the Greek inquisitive crowd, and was essentially Athenian in conduct and in spirit. Indeed, it was more—it was intensely human!

In the Greek tragedies the 'chorus' is a group of characters who represent the ordinary people in their attitudes to the action, which they witness as bystanders, and on which they comment. They often represent the collective community, but not necessarily the poet's thoughts. They expressed traditional, moral, religious, and social attitudes, and were a kind of voice for the audience on stage but in most Greek plays the chorus consists of subsidiary figures who comment rather helplessly on what is happening to the important people. The Greek chorus, it is often said, is a sort of middleman between the unusual main figures and the humdrum spectators.

In the best of the Greek tragedies the chorus comes in at a crucial point of the tragedy, at a time when a lot of pent up emotions cry for release. The choric odes, thus also act as a lyrical release. As Ronald Peacock says, "Everything in art being a matter of mutual assimilation, the extension of meaning through increased poetic power reacts on the dramatic quality; if verse or poetry, makes the expression of the drama more complete it makes it more dramatic. For all these reasons, we find confirmation in the fact, always assumed but rarely stated, that although verse is not indispensable to fine dramatic art, the greatest plays have nevertheless, been all in verse."[8]

T.S. Eliot also in the *Three Voices of Poetry* (1953) feels that: "not the third voice alone but all three voices are found together in dramatic poetry—the poet's most personal expressions when he talks to himself, the poet's remarks with his mask and costume on, and the speeches of characters given a separate identity by the author. Eliot concludes with the statement that, *'The world of a great poetic dramatist is a world in which the creator is everywhere present, and everywhere hidden.'*"[9]

Thus the use of the chorus in drama adds a new dimension to the theatre. Besides being a narrator, a commentator, an expositor and a mediator in the play, it presents the action in its relevant perspective. By its participatory function it gets organically fused into the texture of the play and becomes an inseparable part of the action. It advises, it instructs, it warns and at times even rebukes the protagonist, thus giving a direction to the action of the play. It also expounds the past, comments on the present and illuminates the future. It provides the spectator with a counterpart of himself and in this way the audience sees the action doubly, by seeing its effect on other people. It also presents the inside permutations of the protagonist, playing the role of the Shakespearean soliloquy, depicting the internal conflict of the characters. It also represents the conscience of the community and by its comments presents the verdict of history on the action of the play. And last but not least, it represents the Third Voice of the poet and infuses into the play a poetic sensibility providing an emotional release to the pent up feelings. It also enriches the play with its musical rhythm and dancing patterns giving a fuller expression to the dramatic art, providing the play an added dignity and grandeur. It can do all this and even much more in the hands of a deft artist and a great dramatist. Thus, chorus in drama has a mighty potential which can be clearly seen by a study of its uses through the ages.

(B) ORIGIN AND DEVELOPMENT OF CHORUS IN ANCIENT DRAMA

While tracing the origin and evolution of the chorus as a dramatic convention, when F.L. Lucas said, "Conventions in Art are born rather than made,"[10] he was probably hinting at the evolution of "this relic of primitive religion"[11] as he calls it, from the primitive customs and rituals prevalent in the distant past. These choral odes, which were born from an elemental dramatic rite were a sort of a communal activity, and were very popular amongst the primitive peoples. According to C.M. Bowra, these choral odes "represent an entirely communal state of mind... common consciousness, based on a common purpose."[12] He has further developed this argument in his book *Primitive Song* as follows:

> "Primitive song, which is born from an elemental dramatic rite, is a communal activity. In a world where ceremonies provide a main focus for social life, song is among the chief of them and is used both to communicate with the supernatural and to express joy or grief or other strong emotions. Choral song is the more popular form in most primitive societies. It is, therefore, to some degree, the voice

of the common consciousness, of what a whole society or a representative part of it feels on certain occasions, and we have no reason to doubt that it really does this, or that all its participants share its moods and accept its assumptions."[13]

Thus for any proper and systematic study of the chorus as a dramatic convention, we will have trace its origin from the temple of Dionysus, along with its dithyrambic association, because from its very inception the Greek chorus had been a part of a religious festival, or it may better be called a social ritual (because the word *Religious* is likely to be misleading to the modern ears). Aristotle has also told us that the art of tragedy was derived from the leader of the dithyramb. This dithyramb had had a long history and a wide distribution. Although some writers attribute it to Arion, "who", says Herodotus, "was the first man, of whom we have any knowledge, to compose, name or produce a dithyramb in Corinth."[14] Before Arion this dithyramb was only some sort of choral dance, which formed a part of the Dionysiac ritual. This ritual origin of the dithyramb has been analysed in great details by George Thompson, in *Aeschylus and Athens*—a study in the social origins of the drama. He says:

"It appears, therefore, that the dithyramb had originally belonged to the Dionysiac 'thiasos'[15] of women. The first stage in its evolution as an art form was the decline of the 'thiasos', which followed the declining social status of women. The second stage was reached, when instead of being sung as a processional, it was brought to a stand at an altar and so became a 'stasimon' or standing song—a 'station', in fact...the theme of this stasimon...must have been, in the first instance, the myth corresponding to the rite which was about to be celebrated—the passion of Dionysus. And finally, since there is reason to think that the leader impersonated the god, it is plain that we have here the germ of the ritual drama. When the leader of the dithyramb begins to speak in character to his chorus, the dithyramb is becoming a passion play.... Thus looking back, we may say definitely that the art of tragedy was descended, remotely

Introduction

but directly...from the mimetic rite of the primitive totemic clan."[16]

This ritual pattern of the drama also imposed on the exponents a severe artistic discipline, which gives them strength and solidity, "Varied and often violent emotions which inspire it are subjected to discipline and are made to obey the ideal of shapeliness and harmony."[17] Accordingly, dithyramb also, at the time of Arion and other Dorians was a choral ode sung in honour of Dionysus, set to a brisk kind of music and sung by a troop of fifty satyrs as they danced and gesticulated round the sacrificial alter. The leader of the dithyramb occasionally mounted on the platform and carried a 'dialogue' with other members of the chorus. The subject of the dialogue used to be adventures of Dionysus and their purpose was to explain and amplify the narrative contained in the choral songs.

Dionysus was a nature god, connected particularly, though not exclusively with wine. As a Nature God, he died and was reborn each year and the worship of Dionysus celebrated the rebirth of the God in Spring and his death in Autumn and so the developing art of drama was at times serious and at times comic.

Vaughan, analyzing the various types of tragic drama, says: "In the beginning, the performances of the Greek stage, were, in truth, entirely un-dramatic. In the first instance it would seem, there were no actors at all. The chorus supplied the only personages of the piece; and the chorus acted, in the strictest sense, as a collective body, whose function was to sing hymns... often woven around the tale of some mythical or national hero in honour of Dionysus. It is manifest that we have here nothing that can fairly be called drama. The first step away from this purely ritual performance was taken, as some critics suppose, when one member of the Chorus, the leader perhaps, was detached from the rest and a kind of antiphon instituted between him and them. Such was, or may have been, the beginning of dialogue."[18]

This in a way marks the beginning of the Greek tragic drama wherein the chorus played a very important part. This 'stage-army' was used by earlier dramatists to meet several ends.

According to F.L. Lucas, "It can expound the past, comment on the present and forebode the future. It provides the poet with a mouthpiece and the spectator with a counterpart of himself. It forms a living foreground of common humanity...(sometimes) severing the drama like a magic circle from the real world and (sometimes) providing a bridge between the heroic figures of legend and the average humanity of the audience."[19]

In the midst of such a ritual, some innovator, Thespis, it is said, introduced the first 'actor', as distinct from the choral leader. The object of employing this additional performer was to give greater prominence and effect to the interludes or spoken conversation, with which the lyrical part of the dithyramb was diversified, by transferring them from the choristers, by whom they had hitherto been carried on, to the leader of the chorus and to the actor. This innovation of Thespis was vital and far-reaching in its results. It brought out the performance from the realm of narrative poetry to the dramatic poetry. As F.L. Lucas says: "The leaven of drama began to work and then Aeschylus brought forth the second actor, and later with Sophocles came the third, at which the Greek Tragedy mysteriously stopped. Thus with the development of dramatic art the battle of the Individual against the Group, of the One against the Many started."[20]

"Before any extant drama was composed, a second step had already been taken. There was now one perfectly distinct and separate actor upon the stage, and he carried on a formal and regular dialogue with the chorus; the chorus on its side taking a more specific, a more equal—one might say, a more dramatic part in the action than was subsequently the case."[21] Thus the early drama, which evolved, is often compared to Oratorio and indeed it must have consisted very largely of singing and dancing with the very simplest and shortest of plots, but obviously it would be intensely dramatic. Originally a play was a series of choral odes on a dramatic theme, punctuated by histrionic interludes called episodes. The dramatic action was amplified in the successive odes, which knit the play together.

The play usually began with the entrance of the chorus called the *Parados* and as the histrionic element increased in significance there was prefixed to the *Parados* a scene for the actor or actors, this was called the Prologos. As the tragedy became more realistic the formal Parados was replaced by lyrical conversation between members of the incoming chorus or between the chorus and the actor on the stage. Formal odes after the Parados were later given the name of *Stasimon*. Everything that followed the last stasimon was called the Exodos, i.e. Exit.

Centuries passed by and the importance of the chorus in the plays tended to dwindle in quantity and often in quality also. Thus the history of the chorus in Greek Drama from the times of Thespis right up to Euripides and even after—is a history of gradual decay.

With the development of the histrionic element in drama, chorus gradually lost its primacy. Its former position of a leading agent in the plot was exchanged for the passive role of a spectator. In the earliest period when both tragedy and comedy were mainly lyrical, the members of the chorus were the sole performers. After the introduction of the actors and the dialogues, the chorus still continued for a time to play a leading part. But from the beginning of the 5th century it began slowly to dwindle in importance until it was reduced to the position of an Interlude, which at times had even no connection with the main plot.

It is interesting to watch in the career of Aeschylus himself, how the center of interest was transferred from the orchestra to the stage. The introduction of a second actor naturally led to a complete change in the composition of tragedy, and was no less momentous in its results than the introduction of the first actor by Thespis. "The chorus, now being no longer necessary to the conduct of the piece, steadily declined in importance. Its former position of a leading agent in the plot was gradually exchanged for the passive role of a spectator."[22] On comparing the individual plays together we perceive the dramatic element slowly encroaching upon the lyrical and the significance of the chorus diminishes.

In what seems to be the first extant play of Aeschylus—*The Supplices*, the chorus monopolises the attention of the audience. "*The Supplices* is extremely close to the original choric or communal dance out of which the Tragedy arose.... In it there are really no actors at all, but only three choruses with their respective directors or 'Exarchontes'—Danaus and his daughters, the King of Argive soldiers and the Herald with his swarm of Black Slaves. It consists in the manoeuvring or interaction of the three choruses and their leaders"[23] that the tragedy developed.

It is, however, hardly accidental that both the daughters of Danaus and the sons of Aegyptus are fifty in number. But in *The Persians* we find the number fifty reduced to mere twelve. However, these Persian elders though thinned in number remain august figures full of pomp and dignity of the gorgeous East. "The Persae and Septem are the tragedies, which occupy an intermediate place, between *The Supplices* and later compositions.... In them the chorus still has an intimate connection with the plot.... But in neither of them is the interest concentrated on the chorus, as in *The Supplices*. Moreover the choral odes are greatly reduced in length, and the dialogue proportionately increased."[24]

The Prometheus, one of the poet's latest productions, shows a considerable advance. Here the choral part is reduced to very small dimensions. "But more significant than the mere length of the choral odes is the fact that the Chorus now for the first time begins to assume that conventional and subordinate role which it fills in the dramas of Sophocles and Euripides. It no longer possesses any personal interest or concern in the evolution of the plot, but simply acts as a part of a sympathetic witness, offering advice and consolation to the principal character, and filling up the pauses in the action with general reflections upon the events, which have taken place."[25] In this play we watch the actual crisis, and witness the struggle with our own eyes, instead of being told of it second hand. The dialogue as a rule is marked by intense life and movement and dramatic force. A third actor is occasionally employed, after the fashion set by Sophocles and adds much to the variety and interest of action on the stage.

In the three plays, which compose the *Orestean* trilogy, dramatic representation seems to be much more fully realized than in the prometheus. The chorus, also in two at least of the three plays, occupies the same subordinate place as in the prometheus; and the elders in the agamemnon and the maidens in the choephori, have only a remote connection with the plot. In the eumenides, it is true, the chorus of the Furies plays a much more significant part, and their hostility to Orestes forms the basis of tragedy. But even here the main action takes place upon the stage; and the prominence it gives to the actor's parts—is much greater than would have been the case if the play had been written at an earlier date. "But inspite of its general maturity of dramatic style the *orestea* has still many points in common with the antique kind of drama.... Again in all the three plays, the frequency of the dialogue between the actor and chorus is very noticeable. It appears then from these examples that Aeschylus, even in his latest tragedies, still clung in many instances to the old form,"[26] giving greater prominence to the chorus than what we find in the plays of Sophocles and Euripides.

The rise of Sophocles brings us to the third great epoch in the development of Greek tragedy. "As regards the form of tragedy, the principal novelty introduced by Sophocles was the addition of the third actor. This innovation completed the process which had begun with Aeschylus, and finally put an end to the long contest for supremacy between the actors and the chorus."[27]

With the introduction of the third actor the dramatist was enabled for the first time to confine the dialogue more exclusive to the stage. As a consequence the chorus lost more and more of its significance. The old conversation between the actor and the chorus tended to disappear, and the choral odes were treated as so many resting places in the progress of action. Other significant changes introduced by Sophocles are the abandonment of the trilogy system of composition, and raising the number of the chorus from twelve to fifteen, which must have led to certain modifications in the style of dancing.

The chorus which in Aeschylus was a flexible institution, in Sophocles acquires a fixed and permanent position, and continually reappears in the same stereotyped form. It is not only curtailed in size, but also gradually loses its individuality. The utterances of the chorus now become cool, and sober reflections rather than violent personal passion. It now stands aloof from the stress and storm of the action and assumes the office of an impartial mediator. It is finally excluded from any real share in the action. "Chorus in Sophocles is not an effective agent in the plot. Its position is that of a witness, sympathetic in temper, but undisturbed by anxiety for its own fate.... It never indulges in frantic outbursts of terror, as in the *septem*; or in ejaculation of extreme despair, as in the personae or a malignant revenge as in the Eumenides."[28]

"The office of the Sophoclean chorus, when sharing in the dialogue is to represent the ordinary mass of human beings, as opposed to the heroic figures on the stage. On such occasions there seems to be nothing ideal in its character. It behaves like an average crowd of respectable citizens. It shows no special insight, and is also at times deceived like every one else, as by the pretended repentance of Ajax.... It is also not always averse to fraud, just as after the deception is practiced on Philoctetes, it urges Neoptolenus to commission of still further treachery. As a rule, however, it is pious and god-fearing...but is prevented from giving full expression to its better feelings by excessive caution and timidity.... For example it hesitates to commiserate with Electra, till assured of the King's absence, and though approving of Antigone's action in its heart, is silent through fear.... But when the actors have retired from the stage, and the chorus is left alone to its meditations, it soars to a much higher level, and speaks in a very different strain. It then becomes as it were the mouthpiece of the poet and reveals the moral of the play."[29]

Aristotle, referring to the subject in the *poetics* has one remark, which calls for explanation. He declares that the chorus ought to "form a part of the whole and to join in the action, as in Sophocles, and not as in Euripides."[30] But as Prof. Haigh says, "it is hardly true to say that the chorus of Sophocles takes any practical share in the action. It never plays a part comparable to its part in the supplices or in the euminides in Aeschylus. But such active participation in the events of the drama was altogether antiquated in the times of Aristotle, and lay beyond the range of his speculations. All that he apparently meant by joining in the action was that the choral odes could refer to the

Introduction

subject of the plot, and should not be mere digressions. From this point of view his description of Sophoclean chorus is perfectly accurate."[31]

With the further development of tragedy, it could hardly be expected that along with other alterations introduced by Euripides, the position of the chorus should remain unaffected. "Owing to the increased complexity of the plot it began to be felt as a positive encumbrance.... The chorus in its old shape had become completely incompatible, and as such in course its status was transformed. It was gradually excluded from all real participation in the plot, and its duties were confined in the main to the provision of a musical interlude during the successive scenes."[32] There is a manifest tendency to thrust the chorus more and more into the background. It no longer appears to be deeply affected by the varying fortunes of the drama. Their attitude is less sympathetic and instead of expression of emotion or pensive mediations, they occupy the pauses of the play with long and ornate descriptions of some legendary event.

"A further symptom of the decline of the chorus, and of its gradual conversion into a musical Interlude, is to be found in the style and language of the choral odes. The earlier lyrics of Euripides are masterpieces of graceful beauty and imaginative power but in those, which belong to his later period the execution, on the whole is far less perfect. In spite of numerous brilliant exceptions there is a general tendency, in these later compositions, to subordinate sense to sound, and to think more of the music than of the language. The meaning is occasionally almost lost in the labyrinth of words, which recalls the inanities of the Italian opera."[33]

Speaking generally, then, "the history of the chorus in Euripides, is a history of gradual decline.... But at times even in his later works, Euripides restores chorus to much of its original grandeur and significance.... The most conspicuous example of all this is the *bacchae*. In this play, one of the latest of extant Greek tragedies, the chorus appears to make its dying effort."[34]

Turning our attention from tragedy to comedy we find that the fate of the comic chorus has been much similar. In the beginning here too the chorus formed an integral part of the play. Like tragedy, it was also a blend of two elements, the choral and the histrionic. There is, on the one hand, a succession of scenes in which form is strict; the chorus enters; there is dispute between the chorus and the actor, or between actors, each supported by a semi-chorus; there is formal 'contest' or debate; and finally an address made by the chorus direct to the audience (the Para basis—coming forward).

"The chorus helped throughout the play by naming new characters and commenting on their action. Their presence was particularly helpful because they could entertain the spectators with singing and dancing, a pleasant contrast to the comic scenes of action and repartee, while important events were happening off-stage. In reverse, the chorus occasionally was busy off-stage while the actors amused the audience."[35] But gradually this important participation by the chorus in the comedies also declined.

Looking at the extant plays of Aristophanes, we find that in the first nine of them, which were all produced in the fifth century B.C., the chorus is an important and conspicuous element. But particularly in the later two plays the *ecclesiazusae* (Women in Parliament), which was brought out in 392 B.C. and in *plutos* (Wealth) produced in 388 B.C. there is a great change. The Parabasis had disappeared, and the functions of the chorus are mainly confined to the singing of three or four odes, of no great length. In *plutos*, particularly the decline of the chorus is much more marked. It has only about forty lines assigned to it in the course of the dialogue; and in the pauses between the dialogues; it sang Interludes unconnected with the plot.

During the rest of the century the comic chorus seems to have still lingered on in a position similar to that which it holds in the *plutos*. In the New Comedy of Menander and Philemon, although it seems to have been retained, yet it simply serves the purpose of providing Interludes. A drama which dealt exclusively with the fortunes of private individuals obviously left no room for a chorus, which must in some sense represent the community. Accordingly Menander's chorus is nothing but a group of singers and dancers, who provide breaks between the acts. Sometimes they are dramatically explained away as a bank of tipsy revelers. Their songs are quite irrelevant to the play; in the *Paparus* there is only a heading, "Something for the chorus."

As we come down to the Roman theatre, we find that Roman drama was produced by a succession of writers who strove to adapt Greek originals to native taste for rhetoric, spectacle, sentimentalism and also for homely wit, buffoonery, and biting repartee. Attempts at original composition consisted of a very few plays on Roman historical themes, and a considerable number of comedies on middle class or humble life of Italy. Only in case of Terence can we discern a conscious artistic impulse to improve the Greek model. But one distinctive feature of the Roman stage was that from the very beginning its interest lay not on the orchestra, but on the raised stage on which all the performers appeared. The orchestra immediately in front of the stage remained unused except to accommodate distinguished spectators. Hence the chorus in these Latin adaptations of the Greek plays was probably represented by a single speaker attended perhaps by mutes, who appeared on the stage with other actors. Although this was more realistic yet it changed the native structure and form of the chorus, which in its original form seems to have disappeared with the New Comedy of the Greeks. It was not revived as an independent institution by Romans, and it did not find any place on the stage except in the form of some Interludes between the acts of the drama.

Roman writers like Seneca although retained a chorus, yet in retaining it they carried to further limits the trend already noted in the works of Sophocles and more particularly of Euripides. The choral odes in the tragedies, some of them gifted with cold loveliness are generally unrelated, to the events narrated in the main action. Fundamentally the chorus has now become merely a purveyor of Interludes.

Summing up this gradual decline F.L. Lucas has beautifully said, "The characters in Aeschylus had been colossi, and even his choruses of heroic stature; the characters of Sophocles heroic, his choruses simply human; the characters of Euripides become human, his choruses half ghosts.... After this it is only its bare, disheveled ghost that wails between the acts of the tragedies in Seneca. The chorus that once had unified plays now serves to divide them into acts."[36]

(C) CHORUS IN MEDIEVAL DRAMA: MYSTERIES, MIRACLES AND INTERLUDES

After the decline of the Roman stage, during the Middle Ages the drama underwent a period of eclipse. There was no formal stage for a long time. But during this period the audience were fairly catered by various ritual performances at village festivals, which contributed to the development of the later drama. Such performances included traditional games, festivals, the St. George and the Dragon mummeries, the Sword and the Maypole dances, the Hock Tide festival, the Ploughboy dances, the Robinhood plays and the like.[37] Such semi-dramatic performances were very popular among the masses and worked as a substitute for the true drama till the Mysteries and Miracles came to be staged. In the field of theatre and drama there was nothing but an undercurrent of itenerant Mimmes and acrobats, which the Church later on quietly absorbed with its own rituals and thus unconsciously prepared way for the revival of the theatre.

It is, however, an interesting and ironic fact that modern drama in Europe evolved from the services of that Church which had done so much to suppress the last vestiges of the classical drama, and which had throughout the centuries battled with varying success against the manifestations of its secularised offspring. The drama from which originated the Mysteries, Miracles and Interludes, "began in the Church, not in the theatre, in song not in spoken dialogue, in worship not in entertainment...."[38] As Lucas puts it: "From the tomb of Christ, as once perhaps of Dionysus, the drama rises again into life; again ritual becomes art. But no chorus reappears to dance down the dobbled streets of Coventry or Wakefield. The Middle Ages danced even in the churchyard itself; but their dance failed to wed their drama."[39] George Thompson[40] also agrees with the theory of the ritual origin of the drama in England.

Introduction

The ceremonial of the Mass was a highly dramatic spectacle enhanced by ceremonial and symbolic ritual and the use of antiphonal singing.[41] This antiphonal singing leads itself readily to dialogue and so has the germ of drama.[42] In this characteristic type of Roman chant the two halves of the chorus answer one another or the whole choir answers the single voice of the 'cantor' in alternate versicle and response. This antiphonal singing probably owed something to the influence of the Greek tragic chorus. E.K. Chambers says, "...this tradition was possibly not altogether uninfluenced by the tradition of Greek tragic chorus and Jewish Psalmody."[43]

These musical vestiges of the chorus continued to form an important element in the Liturgical Drama. From these, the next stage was to write texts, called generically "tropes"; and towards the end of the 9th century several independent schools of trope writers grew up. These tropes attached themselves in varying degrees to most of the choral portions of the mass. They "were additions to or amplifications of various passages of the authorized liturgy."[44] The accepted theory is that tropes began early in the 8th century with merely musical amplifications recorded in an imperfect system of musical notation called 'meumai.'[45]

By the ninth century a changed dialogue or trope was inserted into the wordless sequence of Easter morning mass. The chorus was divided into two antiphonal groups, with the white winged angels standing guard over Christ's sepulchre on one side and the women who came seeking Christ's body on the other. The angels chanted: "Whom seek ye in the sepulchre, O followers of Christ? and the women or the Marys responded that they came in search of 'Jesus of Nazareth,' who was crucified." Thereupon the angels informed them that he was not here but had risen as he had foretold, and commanded them to "Go and announce that he is risen from the sepulchre." The news was greeted with inexpressible joy, and the entire congregation rang out with glorious 'To Deum' that followed. This is the content of the earliest preserved text, the 'Quem Quaeritis' trope found at St. Gall. More interesting are the Introit tropes, wherein antiphons and songs are sung to the choir at the beginning of the Mass, as the celebrant approaches the altar. Several of these Introit tropes take a dialogue form, and as in the 'Quem Quaeritis,' they tend to follow in part the 'stichomythia' of the Greek chorus. The Easter trope, thus, grew into a liturgical play.[46]

The eventual development of the tropes or additions to the liturgical chant of the Medieval Church, into the Miracle plays resulted in the introduction of songs of lamentation, of new characters, and of traces in the use of vernacular interpolated in the performances still chanted (almost never spoken) in Latin. Contemporaneously, biblical apocryphal scenes; the performances not only move out of the Church into the churchyard, but also crossed the square into the tavern yard; the actors, previously priests, boys and occasionally nuns, began to obtain the assistance of the lay talent. Plays grew into cycles which serially told the story from the Creation to the Day of Judgment; annual dramatic performances, lasting three or four days, were instituted; and finally the presentation of collective pageant was taken over by the town guilds, each of which made itself responsible for the episode in the connected cycle.

Thus with the transference of the drama from the Church to the laity, regular mysteries and miracle plays began to flow in regularly, in the form of certain cycles. In the extant plays of the various cycles the choric tradition finds its place in a different form. There is the complete and conspicuous absence of the chorus in its physical form, in the drama, but the functional aspect of the chorus can be traced out here and there. These choric devices in the form of Prologue and Epilogue through which the dramatist continues to work as the conscience keeper of the community are to be found in almost all the important plays.

The Messenger in *Everyman*, as also in some of the Chester plays like *The Sacrifice of Isaac*, reads out the Prologue and the Epilogue is sung by the 'Doctour' or the 'Expositor,' who expounds the moral of the performance. In the Moralities their place is also sometimes taken by one of the various characters, as Good Deeds in *Everyman*. These Prologues and Epilogues or the devices of some characters performing the choric function was later adopted by Shakespeare and other Renaissance-dramatists. Except for these unimportant choric devices in the early drama of England, we would but labour in vain to find out any other vestiges of the Greek chorus or any of its adaptations in a newer form.

(D) CHORUS IN RENAISSANCE DRAMA

From the symbolism of the morality plays as the drama moved towards the Realism in Comedy and in Tragedy we again find a trend amongst the dramatists to turn to the classical for guidance. The Renaissance seemed to accelerate this tendency for the revival of interest in the Classical Drama. It was trying to impose a learned tradition upon the native tradition. As such this struggle between the Classicists and the Dramatists holding to the native tradition colours the whole works of the following period, and corresponds to the types of dramatic performance. In some of them, however, there were attempts made to fuse the two into one.

While we turn to the dramatists who were trying to seek inspiration from the Classical drama we find that their models lay in Rome rather than in Greece. It was more or less the influence of Seneca, Terence and other Roman playwrights that was working on the Renaissance Drama of England. The main reason for the common adoption of the Senecan tradition as standard by the Renaissance Dramatists was no doubt the very simple fact that they were much more familiar with Latin than with Greek. Even the Greek masters were available to them in Latin translations, and so even when they were found imitating the Greek plays it was indirectly through the medium of Latin translations which itself accounts for the great difference it made. It accounts for the special technique and structure that was evolved out by the earlier English dramatists and later brought to perfection by the University Wits and finally by Shakespeare. Thus with the rediscovery of the ancient world, although the learned dramatists tried to recapture the secrets of the tragic chorus yet it was imitated more from the Roman masters, where it already existed in a decayed form.

Thus in some of the earlier Elizabethan tragedies where chorus was adopted, it was simply a reproduction of the Senecan chorus, between the Acts. In *Gorbuduc* for instance we have a chorus of 'Foure aunciest and sage men of Brittaine' who do not have any connection with the plot of the play. The chorus probably remains on the stage during the entire performance of the tragedy, and is borrowed directly from Seneca. As far as its proper function as chorus goes it is purely formal. In fact it is much more detached from the action than in any of the Senecan plays. Its expression is confined to the utterances of moral platitudes suggested by the misfortunes of the characters in the main action. Further, in *Gorbuduc*, however, the chorus performs the function of expounding to the audience at the end of the act the significance of the pantomime presented at the beginning of the act. This scheme was completely new, for which no precedent is known.

The same scheme was also adopted by Kyd in his *Spanish Tragedy* at the end of the Third Act, where a dumb show appears. In *Spanish Tragedy* we have the ghost of a dead man and Revenge, together playing the role of Senecan chorus. They convey an eerie feeling of the insignificance of human actors against the timeless background of the dead. But in spite of the abstract chorus of these supernatural spirits, we cannot compare it to *Eumenides*, because of the helplessness with which they watch the movement of the play, inspite of their being so deeply interested in the events. They enter the stage just in the beginning and Revenge concludes the first act by singing:

"Here we sit down to see the mystery,
And serve for chorus in the tragedy."

Then at the end of every act there is one complete scene allotted to the chorus, where the Ghost of Andrea and Revenge talk to each other commenting on the passing events from the vantage position of a supernatural.

Again in Jocasta (jointly translated and produced by Gascoigne and Kinwelmersh), there is a chorus of 'foure Thebane dames'. Although the play claims to be the first English translation of the Greek play written by Euripides, yet as some

Introduction

critics have observed, it is probably a paraphrase of Dolce's *Giocasta*, although the main line of action laid down by Euripides in the *Phoenissae* has been followed by the translators. The four Theban dames which form the chorus remain on the stage from the entrance in the first act to the end of the tragedy. But some of the beautiful odes spoken by the chorus in the Greek play have been neglected by the translators and some other substitutes are found in their place newly written by the translators. It has somewhat marred the beauty and grandeur of the play. But it is just possible the translators must have thought the mythological allusions in Greek chorus, too remote and unintelligible, perhaps too cumbersome to be exhibited in English. Even the translation of some of the choric odes is very loose and unimpressive. But the explanation can be traced in the fact that Gascoigne submissively followed Dolce and not so much Euripides.

In yet another translation of a play by Seneca *Thyrestes*, by J. Haywood, we find the same Roman tradition faithfully adopted. There is a chorus, but it is, however, not specified as to who is to act as chorus. This makes the things all the more detached and impersonal. This chorus appears at the end of each act, but for the Fourth Act which has only one scene. This whole scene is utilised by the chorus in its talk with the Messenger who appears on the scene in the classical tradition.

Besides this, there are numerous classical tragedies in which we have chorus but following the Roman model rather than the Greek one. We also have a similar chorus in Marlowe's *Dr. Faustus*, which has been assigned the role of speaking the Prologue and the Epilogue, and appears at times between the acts. Its function is also the making of moralising comments, and it stands detached and helplessly aloof from the plot. But some of its utterances are highly poetical, and display Marlowe's genius as a poet.

In Shakespeare, although there is a conspicuous absence of chorus in his plays, yet in *Henry V* we find Shakespeare also using this ancient instrument in the typical Roman fashion, by placing the chorus between the acts of the drama. Besides providing the tragic relief in the play, it has also helped

Shakespeare in maintaining the unity of Time and Place by bridging over the gaps of time:

"And the scene
 Is now transported, gentles, to Southampton;
 There is the playhouse now, there must you sit:
 And thence to France shall we convey you sage,
 And bring you back, charming the narrow seas
 To give you gentle pass;...."[47]

The chorus in the play is also helpful in interpreting matter which cannot be presented dramatically due to the limitations of Shakespearean stage. The contending elements in the drama are gigantic and heroic, that the stage cannot represent them, and so the imaginative guidance by the chorus has to 'piece out' the actor's imperfections. It thus makes a deliberate appeal to the imagination of the audience. The chorus speaks out more than 200 lines throughout the play and is probably the solitary example in Shakespeare where the chorus so materially furthers the progress of the story. Then there are certain other plays of Shakespeare wherein certain characters are allocated to play the role of chorus. In *Pericles*, for instance, we have Gower acting as chorus, or Time as chorus in *The Winter's Tale*. Otherwise we find that Shakespeare like so many other Renaissance dramatists has neglected the ancient institution of the chorus and has evolved out a structure wherein there was neither any scope nor any place for chorus to play an important part.

Accounting for the decline of the chorus in the Middle Ages and later in the Elizabethan Age, Nicoll holds that it was not necessary for the expression of true tragic emotions.[48] Gray also in his letter to Mason expresses almost the same opinion in the following words: "A greater liberty in the choice of the fables and the conduct of it, was the necessary consequence of retrenching the Chorus. Love and Tenderness delight in privacy. The soft effusions of the soul, Mr. Mason, would not bear the presence of the gaping, singing, and dancing, moralising, uninterested crowd...."[49] And as it is true of Love, so is it true of every passion which is checked and cooled by the 'fiddling crew.'

Moreover, the Humanist and the Individualist trend during the Elizabethan Age also explains the absence of the chorus in the Renaissance drama, which was based on the glorification of human personality and as such there was no need for this dramatic convention which represented the community and formed the essential basis of the Classical Tragedy of Greece.

Although the chorus is not present in most of the Elizabethan plays, yet their success lay not in resurrecting the ancient convention, but in inventing other ways of doing what it had done. For if the popular Elizabethan playwright had no chorus, on the other hand he could have on the stage at once not three characters only, but almost as many as he chose. And a single one of them, like Enobarbus in *Antony and Cleopatra* might suffice by himself to do much of the work, the chorus once performed. We have such character-choruses in other plays also, as Horatio in *Hamlet*. Then practically the Shakespearean Fool, as in *King Lear* or Touchstone in *As You Like It* or Feste in *The Winters Tale* have always the choric function to perform. There are also some scenes in Shakespeare which serve as a substitute for the chorus. The grave-diggers' scene in *Hamlet* is an example of such a technique. The soliloquies is yet another device which Renaissance dramatists use to their own advantages in analysing the inner conflicts of the character's mind. This technique had a special advantage over chorus. Then the song element in Shakespearean Drama also compensates for the absence of the chorus of providing the lyrical element in the play, which was one of the chief functions of the chorus itself.

All this is indicative of the fact that the Renaissance dramatists had developed an altogether new type of dramatic structure, different from the classical one, wherein chorus had no place. They, however, had so many other devices to compensate for the absence of this ancient convention. As F.L. Lucas says, "Where the Greek chorus served as a foil, a type of common humanity beside the heroic figures of legend, the Shakespearean stage has its meaner characters, its citizens, its crowds, its clowns. Where the Greek chorus provided a lyric relief for tragic tension, Elizabethan dramatists have on the one hand the laughter of their fools, on the other the lyric beauty of their stage-songs and the poetry they can put in the mouth of almost any character, however sordid or villainous."[50]

(E) REVIVAL OF THE GREEK MODEL IN *SAMSON AGONISTES*

The credit, however, goes to Milton for reviving the Greek form of drama for the first time in English literature with the chorus as the central convention. The experiment conducted by Milton, in his *Samson Agonistes*, is significant and remarkable in the field. Having been written on the model for classical Greek tragedy, it is not divided into acts, but the divisions are on the basis of the choral odes. In the 'Parodos' the chorus imparts to the audience the previous history of Samson and underlines the contrast between what he is and what he once was, and fills us with a sense at once, of his greatness and weakness, the fatal rift that ruins all.

Then later when Samson refuses the proposal of ransom made by Manoah, the chorus seeks to cheer him, and also tries to console him at his unfortunate lot. It also tries to calm the indignation of Samson after the stormy scene with Haropha. It tries to persuade him to obey the civil authority. So long as Samson is on the stage, it serves to illustrate his character partly by contrast and partly by sympathy. And finally when the catastrophe is announced the chorus in a most beautiful simile shows that the death of Samson has fulfilled the work to which his life had been consecrated; and draws the moral by saying—"All is best, though we oft doubted what the unsearchable dispose of Highest wisdom brings about...."[51]

Thus we find the chorus which remains on the stage from the beginning to the end of the play, and performs the main function which in the words of Arnold are, "To combine, to harmonise, to deepen for the spectator the feeling naturally excited in him by the sight of what was passing upon the stage—this is the one grand effect produced by the chorus in Greek tragedy."[52] The chorus in *Samson Agonistes* conforms to that high standard. It has also helped Milton in maintaining the unities of Time and Place, as is claimed by Milton himself. The circumscription of time wherein the whole drama begins and ends is according to ancient rule and best example, within the space of twenty-four hours.

Thus the chorus occupies an important place in the structure of the drama. It is a sharer in the action of the play. In grandeur and loftiness *Samson Agonistes* approaches the Aeschylean drama. In the conduct of his chorus Milton is even superior to Euripides, whose choruses indulge in sententious maxims and wordy declamations, too often irrelevant and wide off the mark.

Explaining measure of verse used by him in the chorus Milton himself has written: "The measure of verse used in the chorus is of all sorts, called by the Greeks Monostrophic, or rather 'Apolelymenon' without regard had to Strophe, Antistrophe, or Epode, which were a kind of stanzas framed only for the music then used with the chorus that sung; not essential to the poem, and therefore not material; or being divided into stanzas or pauses, they may be called Alloeostropha."

Thus in the verse form Milton has followed Euripides, whose choruses are constructed on the relaxed monostrophic principles. The metre that Milton has adopted is Blank Verse of five feet in each line. And each foot is an Iambus. This is known as the Heroic Blank Verse. There are, however, many variations, but this is usually the normal order. Milton was against the use of rhyme in verse, as he says in his Prefatory note to *Paradise Lost*. "...rhyme being no necessary adjunct of the ornament of poem or good verse, in longer works especially, but the invention of a barbarous age, to set off wretched matter and metre."[53]

But Walter Headlam does not very much appreciate the verse that Milton provides for his chorus, which according to him proves more laborious. According to him rhyme would have added to the charm. "Had Milton known the true construction of Greek Choral Song, we may be sure that instead of mistaken imitations in *Samson Agonistes*, he would have given us inventions no less beautiful than the stanzas of *Hymn to Nativity*...."[54]

Milton, thus, in *Samson Agonistes*, has reproduced with rigid fidelity its form, and has succeeded in showing how that form may become, even for modern, legitimately and effectively a model. He had, in England several followers, but in the range of both Elizabethan and Restoration drama, he stands unique. This great experiment of Milton stands out as solitary in their midst, as Milton himself in England of Restoration or Samson amongst the Philistines.

The chorus of *Samson Agonistes* is, like its Sophoclean prototype, excluded from any important share in the action. The chorus does play certain part in the hero's regeneration but this influence is comparatively slight. Instead of comforting Samson, they are soon led to echo his despair. The trait is thoroughly Sophoclean. So the other functions of the chorus, like representing the common aspects of morality, consoling the afflicted hero, and cautioning against oppression and finally acting as a spokesman of the dramatist are, however, on a feebler note.

(F) USE OF CHORUS IN THE CONTINENTAL DRAMA

On the continent also the attraction for the chorus was quite great. It was used, with great enthusiasm in the Italian, Spanish, French and German literatures. Tasso introduced it in *Torismondo* (1586), and Lope de Vega (1562–1635) in his *Aranco Domado*. It also occurs in French literature in Racine, who has used it in *Esther* (1689) and in *Athalie* (1691). Then it also appears in the works of the great German dramatist Schiller in his *Bride of Messina* (1804), "which in respect of form—the retention, for example, of the chorus—adheres much more closely to the Athenian model than anything produced by Goethe."[55] Besides these significant plays there are a number of other plays wherein this convention has been successfully used.

(G) CHORUS DURING 18TH & 19TH CENTURIES

But in England, after Milton, for a very long time, the chorus was not present even in an indirect way, because the drama was becoming more and more secularised and prosaic in style with a great amount of social criticism and comedy at the expense of individual follies as in the Comedies of Manners and Sentiments.

In the 18th century the physical conditions of the theatre had changed and these changes were unfavourable for the drama. The audience too had changed bringing about a change in the very tone of drama. The first few decades of the century could boast of no remarkable play. Still we find some sporadic attempts wherein chorus find a place. In some of the serious plays, as in Mason's (1724–1797) *Elfrida* (1753) there is a chorus of British virgins and in *Caractacus* (1759) a chorus of Druids and Bards. The conspicuous absence of the chorus in this age, is also due to the fact that the plays in the 18th century had cut themselves off, from the ritual atmosphere from which emanated the Greek and Elizabethan Drama. Moreover, the stage developments were also bringing the audience directly facing the stage, completely eliminating the physical presence of the chorus.

However, during this period, the chorus was going over to the operas and musical comedies. In the operas chorus became one of the most attractive features providing spectacle and musicality. The operatic chorus almost fulfilled the Greek Conventions, and they progressed greatly during the Romantic period. Important among them are Mozart's (1756–1791) *Don Giovanni* and the operas of Handel (1685–1759), who carried choral music to its highest point; and J.S. Bach (1685–1750). The chorus is also present in the light operas like Gay's *Beggar's Opera* (1728)—the chorus of gangsters (Macheath's Gang) and of Women of Town. However, Gay's *The Beggar's Opera* is one of the outstanding achievements of the English stage in the early 18th century.

After the close of the 18th century dawned the Romantic Period, but the Romantic Temper was not so conducive to the kind of objectivity that is required of the dramatist even though the poets were writing in verse. Inspite of this the age was prolific in its output of verse plays, even though most of them remained unacted. As the Romantic poets were remote from the general current of life, they could not give what was wanted on the stage. Consequently their plays had little dramatic merit and dramatic literature was at a low ebb.

The verse dramatists of the nineteenth century had also to struggle against the character of the popular theatre, which was expected to satisfy the demand for spectacle. Abstract ideas have often played a large part in drama. But the important matter is one of stress. When the Romantics attempt to dramatise abstract issues they tend to delineate characters which stand for an ideal rather than portray an individual. The Romantics lacked the dramatic aptitude to create complex characters. The Romantic poets had a fertile imagination, they could visualize characters vividly and their verse also sometimes rise to the occasion, as in the plays of Shelley and Byron. But these poets had no real touch with life nor were they aware of the requirements of the stage or of the need for experiments in dramatic verse showing individuality, so that their plays remain closet dramas or dreams in which the poets express their lyric impulse in a slightly different form.

It was, therefore, left to poets like Shelley and Byron to think of the chorus on a Greek model. They wanted to revive the old form of chorus just as a channel of rescue for saving the English drama from the rut in which it had fallen after the 17th century. But their interest was a sort of an embrionic beginning of experimenting with the form so as to evolve out an entirely new type of drama. They had a powerful predecessor in Milton and were trying to introduce a new set of conventions. During this period we find a chorus of Swinish Multitude in *Oedipus Tyrannus* (1820) and of abstract spirits, elements and symbolic figures like Furies Spirits, and Hours in the *Prometheus Unbound* (1820); and in *Hellas* (1823) we find a chorus of Greek Captive Women. Shelley's chorus fulfils the function of propounding the poet's personal philosophy and gives expression to his lyricism. Had Shelley substituted his chorus of abstracts with concrete characters, he could have succeeded in giving us a new form—workable on the stage. Shelley's *The Cenci* and Keats' *Otho* were based on Elizabethan conventions. Hence apart from certain rich poetic patches they have very little to offer.

Byron had the making of the dramatist in him. His *Manfred* (1817), which resembles Goethe's *Faust*, is considered by some critics to be his weakest play but some of the speeches of the hero show that Byron could endow his characters with a distinct personality. But even Byron's *Manfred* is not free from abstraction. He has also introduced a chorus of Earth Spirits and mortals in his mystery *Heaven and Earth* (1822). Apart from these significant experiments there were not many dramas written with chorus as the central convention.

Thereafter, between the Romantics and the rise of Modern drama, we have a few attempts made in this direction by the Victorians. Like the Romantics, the Victorian poets also lacked the energising influence of a living theatre in which they could learn their craft and see that their production came into their own. This want prevented them, despite their genius from writing drama in the real sense of the term. The Victorian poets Tennyson and Browning also made forays into the sphere of poetic drama like their predecessors, but their spoils were equally sporadic. Robert Browning had a far greater knack of the dramatic than any of the writers mentioned so far and this is revealed in many of his dramatic monologues. Browning can go deep into the psychology of the characters but his play suffers from lack of movement and a too rhetorical dialogue.

The Victorian poets too exprimented with drama. But they were the sort of plays that would not 'act.' They were far too 'literary.' Matthew Arnold and Swinburne evinced a keen interest in Greek drama. Arnold's *Merope* (1858) and Swinburne's *Atalanta in Calydon* (1865) are close imitations of Greek tragedy. As a lyrical drama it is a superb piece of work, which marks out his kinship with Shelley. In 1876 Swinburne published *Erechtheus*, founded on a fragment of Euripides, characterized by the same fine classic spirit which marked the Atlanta, but evincing maturer powers and richer imagination. There is a chorus in Swinburne's *Atalanta in Calydon* (1864) and in *Erechtheus* (1876) there is chorus of Athenian Elders. Then we have Mrs. Browning's *Drama of Exile* (1844), which has the chorus of Eden Spirits and Invisible Angels. But the more important work of this age is Arnold's *Merope* (1858) which has got a chorus of Messonian Maidens and the choric odes are strophic and antistrophic. In the preface to this play, Arnold has also provided significant comments on the need for reviving the chorus in English drama.

(H) REVIVAL OF CHORUS IN MODERN POETIC PLAYS

The most serious attempts, however, at reviving the chorus have been made by those poets and dramatists who have been interested in reviving the poetic drama in modern times. The aim of all these 'poets of the theatre' has been to discover more satisfactory conventions of the play than the traditional Elizabethan way of construction. These poets in reviving poetic drama invariably fell back upon the choric element with some variations in its composition, function and movement on the stage.

"In the eighteen nineties the English theatre was opened to a fresh breeze from Scandinavia; the drama of ideas exemplified in some of the plays of Ibsen is to be seen also as a reaction against naturalism. William Archer translated Ibsen's plays into English, and *Ghosts* was produced in 1891. Subsequently his symbolic and imaginative plays such as *The Master Builder, Peer Gynt* and *The Wild Duck* broke the 'peace of the English theatre' and stimulated a return to poetic drama."[56] This resurgence that was taking place in the drama of this period spread over the whole of Europe—from Ireland in the West to Russia in the East.

In England, however, during the late nineties and with the opening of the twentieth century, we find only a few major adherents of poetic plays. Dramatists like Robert Bridges (1844–1930) and Stephen Philips (1868–1930) were making some humble effort to revive poetic plays with Greek themes. Bridges' experiment in drama from *Prometheus* (1883) to *Demeter* (1905) are to be regarded as an expression of his interest in various forms of drama, particularly the 'mask.' But to him 'mask' means the narration of an old story in poetry. He very faithfully keeps to the form of the Greek play in the matter of using a chorus and a severely limited cast. The lyrical description of the gentle eyed Demeter and the chorus of the

Oceanides contribute to the poetic charm of the play. But Stephen Philips's sense of the theatre gives him a higher place in the hierarchy of drama than Bridges. Philips's first true success came with *Herod* (1900), and then with *Ulysses* (1902), *The Sin of David* (1904) and *Nero* (1906). The Greek myth has always provided him a framework to write. But he never succeeded in applying the Greek myth to a modern situation, as Eliot later succeeded in providing.

Then the verse drama took a new turn with John Davidson and Thomas Hardy (1840–1928). The play of ideas began to invade the realm of poetic drama. These plays were full of ideas but were never produced. Hardy's great epic drama *The Dynasts* was published in three parts—Pt. I-1904; Pt. II-1906; and Pt. III-1908. An epic drama of the war with Napoleon in three parts, nineteen Acts and one hundred and thirty scenes. This great work is mainly in blank verse, partly in a variety of other metres, partly in prose. The introduction of the choruses, the Spirit of the Pieties and the Spirits Ironic and Sinister enables Hardy to avoid involvement in his theme and to have a comparatively detached view of the scenes and to provide commentary on the phenomena of history. Apart from the chorus of Phantasmal Intelligences, Hardy uses a number of other devices, Elizabethan in origin, to give unity to the mass of material he condenses. There are many scenes in prose, which produce a choric effect. The characters use chorus like words, which throw light on the main episodes relating to the more important characters. Hardy's handling of this device is according to Shakespearean fashion.

Meanwhile, by the end of the nineteenth century, the Symbolist movement was holding its sway over the continent and in England. It found its chief exponent in Arthur Symons, who wrote *The Symbolist Movement in Literature*, describing the contribution of Varlaine, Mallarme and Maeterlinck. Maeterlinck (1862–1949), the Belgian poet-dramatist, wrote plays dealing with mystery and 'the interior life' and had nothing to do with the external world. His ideal was 'static' drama with their suggestive power, their haunting mystery and their complete exclusion of the world of humdrum reality. It is, however, no wonder that he provided inspiration to such a playwright as W.B. Yeats.

"Yeats's contribution to the realm of poetic drama was manifold. From the early plays with their trance like atmosphere, their meditative rhythms and their decorative imagery he passed on to the more elaborate characterization and subtler poetic style of plays like 'The King's Threshold' and 'The Hour Glass' and in 'Four Plays for Dancers' he achieved his ideal of the drama as being able to recede from us into some more powerful life."[57] W.B. Yeats in his great effort to revive poetic drama thought of various types of chorus with dancers in his *Four Plays for Dancers* with weird recitative lines. Yeats also introduced the chorus as it is found in the Noh Drama of Japan.

Following Yeats, the same Noh type of chorus has been brought up by Gordon Bottomley especially in his plays like *Marsalli's Weeping*. In some of these plays Bottomley uses the device of curtain folders like Yeats and he also makes use of the chorus to represent certain natural sounds like those of the waves. In *The Singing Sands* there is a chorus of Waves and the chorus of the Snow people. Bottomley's use of a chorus—whether derived from the Noh or Greek drama—is a great contribution to dramatic literature. "He has given us not only poetry which is drama, austere, remote, yet real and beautiful, but something new besides: a form of drama in which for the first time the choruses are the protagonists."[58] In his religious play, *The Acts of St. Peter,* the lines of the chorus describing the supreme moment of Christ on the Cross show the vigour of the verse based on a simple idiom.

Thomas Sturge Moore (1870–1946) also followed the Noh technique of W.B. Yeats with his chorus of Curtain Folders, but he adapts the Noh technique in different ways. Moore was interested in Biblical and classical themes, which provided proper material for his symbolic plays. His contribution to poetic drama may be meager in volume, but he has some importance for his experiments. Before he tried his hand at the Noh technique, using the device of curtain bearing and folding, he had written *Aphrodite Against Artemis* (1901). Later in *Media* (1920) and *Psyche in Hades* (1930) in which he uses the

Noh device, he uses curtain bearing and folding technique to dramatise the story. However, he further modified the Noh technique, in his plays where he does not use the musicians. In *Daimonassa*, a tragedy that is considered the best of Sturge Moore's plays, he uses one aspect of the Noh technique—the musicians with zither, one of the three instruments used by Yeats. The play's interest lies in the dramatist's use of the musicians, who act as Prologue and Chorus as well. However, like Yeats he strove to emphasise the importance of poetry on the stage.

Apart from these exponents, the chorus has been a stock element in all the religious plays of modern times like those of Masefield's *Good Friday* (1917), *The Trial of Jesus* (1923) and *Coming of Christ* (1926). Masefield's religious dramas have a limited appeal, but his endeavour has been to give them universal feeling by clothing the main incidents of the Gospel story in poetry of a high order. Masefield is very close to the classical tradition and his plays are characterized by classical simplicity and adherence to the classical unities. *The Trial of Jesus* is a prose play interspersed with verse spoken by the choruses of men and women, and *The Coming of Christ* is a kind of morality play in which the chorus was accompanied by organ and pianoforte music. The appeal of the play is religious. Abercrombie also in his religious play *The Sale of Saint Thomas* (1930) treats the legend with originality and dignity. The dramatist with his poetical powers and speculative imagination uses his typical blank verse.

In this tradition of poetic plays came the great modern master—T.S. Eliot whose contribution in this field is of immense value. Eliot explored the drama of the Elizabethans and the Ancients and put into it a new sense of renaissance wonder and greatness. In fact the poetic drama began officially in 1932 when *Sweeney Agonistes*—an Aristophanic Melodrama was published. It was followed in 1934 by a pageant play *The Rock* wherein the liturgical element is dominant, especially in the choruses. Then the next year, in 1935, a great modern classic *Murder in the Cathedral* was produced. Its deep spiritual message, the blending of mysticism with realistic humour and its flight of lyrical sublimity made it one of the noblest experiments in poetic drama. In this play there is a chorus of Canterbury Women, whose choric speeches have given the play an entirely new dimension. Eliot, thereafter, made a fresh experiment with the chorus in *The Family Reunion* (1939) which is an even bolder venture. He tried to weave the chorus into the very texture of the play by giving the choric role to some of its characters. But after this play Eliot abandoned the formal use of the chorus in *The Cocktail Party* (1949), *The Confidential Clerk* (1953) and *The Elder Statesman* (1958), but continued to perform the choric function with the help of certain compensatory devices and in this way chorus still formed a part of his plays but appeared with a mask.

Thus, besides giving through his plays new themes and new settings, Eliot has given the poetic drama a new dimension and a new medium. He enlarged the scope of the verse drama. He also developed a verse form suitable for contemporary situations and revitalised the theatre of the day. He revived the Greek convention of the chorus but he did not simply copy the Greeks. He gave the chorus an entirely new dimension by making it an integral part of the play. His major achievement, therefore, is the way he has developed appropriate method to integrate the subject matter of his themes with the dramatic structure of his play.

Eliot's experiments, however, exercised a great influence on other dramatists and chorus emerged as a powerful dramatic convention. His experiments in each of his plays, opened fresh avenues for other dramatists to follow and adapt according to their needs. Christopher Fry whose contribution to modern poetic drama is manifold adapted it into an entirely new path. His sense of the comic and his delight in the mystery and wonder of existence have given a distinctive flavour to his plays. He makes abundant use of figurative language but the metaphors and similes used by him strike us by their unconventionality. Similarly Auden's *Dance of Death* (1933), *The Dog Beneath the Skin* (1935) and *The Ascent of F6* (1936) also reflect the influence of Eliot on his plays and his powerful use of the chorus in them. Similarly Stephen Spender's *The Trial of A Judge*

Introduction

(1938), Ronald Duncan's *This Way to The Tomb* and Norman Nicholson's *The Old Man and the Mountains* have also adapted and used chorus in their poetic plays to suit their purpose. John Gross has admirably summed up our impression of T.S. Eliot's dramatic works: "But what Eliot has left is an example of unwavering artistic integrity, and a glimpse of what might be achieved: enough to persuade any successor that the undertaking is worthwhile."[59]

NOTES AND REFERENCES

1. *Everyman's Encyclopaedia*. 4th Edition, Vol. III. 430.
2. Harvey, Sir Paul. *Oxford Companion to Classical Literature*. 99.
3. Eliot T.S. November 25, 1936. *The Listener*. 995.
4. Sharma, H.L. 1976. *T.S. Eliot—His Dramatic Theories*. New Delhi: S. Chand & Co. 75.
5. *Ibid*. 74-75.
6. Eliot, T.S. 1964. *The Use of Poetry and the Use of Criticism*. London: Faber and Faber. 153.
7. Aristotle. *Poetics*. XVII. 7.
8. Peacock, Ronald. 1957. *The Art of Drama*. London: Routledge & Kegan Paul.
9. Eliot, T.S. *The Three Voices of Poetry*. Quoted in Smith, Carol H. 1963. *T.S. Eliot's Dramatic Theory and Practice*. London: Oxford University Press. 236-37.
10. Lucas, F.L. 2003. *Tragedy*. London: Hoggarth Press, Indian Reprint. New Delhi: A.I.T.B.S. Publishers and Distributors. 82.
11. *Ibid*.
12. Bowra, C.M. 1959. *Primitive Song*. London: Oxford University Press. 32.
13. *Ibid*.
14. Haigh, A.E. 1938. *The Tragic Drama of the Greeks*. Oxford: Clarendon Press. 17.
15. The Dionysiac 'thiasos' was a secret magical society which preserved in modified form the structure and functions of the totemic clan, out of which it had evolved during the later phase of the tribal society. It was composed of women led by a male priest. Its principal rite derived from initiation, contained three elements: an orgiastic exodus into the open country—a sacrament in which a victim was torn to pieces and eaten raw, and a triumphal return. This ritual was projected as a myth of the passion of Dionysus.

16. Thompson, George. 1941. *Aeschylus and Athens*. London: Oxford University Press. 7.
17. Bowra, C.M. 1959. *Primitive Song*. London: Oxford University Press. 32-33.
18. Vaughan. 2004. *Types of Tragic Drama*. Indian Reprint. Meerut: Shalabh Publishing House. 24-25.
19. Lucas, F.L. 2003. *Tragedy*. London: Hoggarth Press. Indian Reprint. New Delhi: A.I.T.B.S Publishers and Distributors. 82-83.
20. *Ibid*. 79-80.
21. Vaughan. 2004. *Types of Tragic Drama*. Indian Reprint. Meerut: Shalabh Publishing House. 25.
22. Haigh, A.E. 1938. *The Tragic Drama of the Greeks*. Oxford: Clarendon Press. 62.
23. Gilbert Murray. *The Complete Plays of Aeschylus*. Introduction.
24. Haigh, A.E. 1938. *The Tragic Drama of the Greeks*. Oxford: Clarendon Press. 63.
25. *Ibid*. 64.
26. *Ibid*. 65.
27. *Ibid*. 137-38.
28. *Ibid*. 152.
29. *Ibid*. 153-54.
30. Aristotle. *Poetics*. XVIII, 7.
31. Haigh, A.E. 1938. *The Tragic Drama of the Greeks*. Oxford: Clarendon Press. 155.
32. *Ibid*. 251-52.
33. *Ibid*. 254.
34. *Ibid*. 256.
35. Lever, Katherine. *The Art of Greek Comedy*. London: Metheun & Co. Ltd. 127.
36. Lucas, F.L. 2003. *Tragedy*. London: Hoggarth Press. Indian Reprint, New Delhi, A.I.T.B.S. Publishers and Distributors. 84-85.
37. A detailed analysis of all these are found in Chambers, E.K. *The Medieval Stage*.
38. Craig, Hardin. 1960. *English Religious Drama of the Middle Ages*. London: Oxford University Press. 1.
39. Lucas, F.L. 2003. *Tragedy*. London: Hoggarth Press. Indian Reprint. New Delhi: A.I.T.B.S. Publishers and Distributors. 86.

40. Thompson, George. 1941. *Aeschylus and Athens*. London: Oxford University Press. 193. (The English Drama had fundamental elements in common with the Greek, for these liturgical plays were influenced by the mumming play, folk dance, and other performances derived from the agrarian ritual of the Germanic tribes....)
41. Craig, Hardin. 1960. *English Religious Drama of the Middle Ages*. London: Oxford University Press. 10. (In religious plays there also appeared from the beginning hymns and antiphons as services pieces, and they no doubt prepared the way for the free use of songs in Elizabethan Drama.)
42. Craig, Hardin. 1960. *English Religious Drama of the Middle Ages*. London: Oxford University Press. 20. (Dialogue is provided for in the liturgy in great abundance. Since not only in antiphons and responses but in recitals of all sorts, singing was responsive—between a single leader and a chorus, between two parts of a divided chorus, or between any parts or groupings called for by the liturgy.)
43. Chambers, E.K. *The Medieval Stage*.
44. Craig, Hardin. 1960. *English Religious Drama of the Middle Ages*. London: Oxford University Press. 30.
45. *Ibid*.
46. Gasner, John. *Masters of Drama*. 3rd revised edition and enlarged. Dover Publications Incorporated. 141.
47. Shakespeare. *Henry V*.
48. Nicoll, A. 1957. *Theory of Drama*. London: George G. Harrap & Co. 159.
49. Toyanbee, P. and Whibley L. (Ed.). 1935, Correspondence i. 358.
50. Lucas, F.L. 2003. *Tragedy*. London: Hoggarth Press. Indian Reprint. New Delhi: A.I.T.B.S. Publishers and Distributors. 88-89.
51. Milton, John. *Samson Agonistes*.
52. Arnold, Matthew. *Merope*. Introduction.
53. Milton, John. *Paradise Lost*. Prefatory Note.
54. Headlam, Walter. 1907. *A Book of Greek Verse*. XVII.
55. Vaughan. 2004. *Types of Tragic Drama*. Indian Reprint. Meerut: Shalabh Publishing House. 225.
56. Gowda, Anniah. 1972. *The Revival of English Poetic Drama*. New Delhi: Orient Longman. 349.
57. Chaturvedi, B.N. 1967. *English Poetic Drama of the Twentieth Century*. Gwalior: Kitab Ghar. 31.
58. Gowda, Anniah. 1972. *The Revival of English Poetic Drama*. New Delhi: Orient Longman. 243-44.

59. Gross, John. 1965, March. *Eliot from Ritual to Realism in Encounter*. Vol. XXIV, No. 3. 50. Quoted in Sarkar, Subhas. 2006. *T.S. Eliot—The Dramatist*. New Delhi: Atlantic Publishers & Distributors (P) Ltd. 290.

2

Sweeney Agonistes and Other Fragments

(A) SWEENEY AGONISTES

Eliot is supposed to have made his debut as a dramatist in *Sweeney Agonistes*—a fragment, although it does not find a place among his plays and was published under the heading 'Unfinished Poems.' 'Fragment of a Prologue' appeared in the *New Criterion* in October 1926. 'Fragment of an Agon' was published in the same magazine in its January issue in 1927, both under the general title of *Wanna Go Home Baby?* The title became *Sweeney Agonistes* when it came out in a book form in 1932.

Sweeney, however, is a familiar figure with Eliot. "From *Sweeney Erect* to *Sweeney Among the Nightingales*, and then to *Sweeney Agonistes*, the Sweeney myth has grown in significance and in potentiality."[1] Sweeney actually is Eliot's characterization of the unrefined, sensual, secular man—a debased and a debauched image of what humanity has ultimately been degraded to. So far the character implicit in the poems is very much in-keeping with the Sweeney of the play. The difference is that the Sweeney presented in the play is no more just a fleeting reference or a passive description or a representative image of modern man but someone who has been given a chance to be articulate, to communicate his ideas, to share his insights, in other words he is an active participator. Sweeney of the poems who represents the shabbiness of the world has become a further developed Sweeney of the play. Since he has been part of the horror and the boredom, his understanding and discernment of the human condition is all the greater. This would also explain Sweeney's motivation to voice (despite his unrefined manner) and share (despite his desolation) his experience with the others.

The 'Agonistes' part of the title immediately suggests *Samson Agonistes* and analogises with both the dilemma of Samson and to the Greek dramatic structure used in Milton's work. Carol H. Smith contends, "Samson's dilemma is that of exile in an alien world who feels compelled by divine will to pull that world down around his own head in order to destroy its iniquities. Sweeney is perhaps another spiritual outcast in a corrupt world, and he too must destroy himself in his attack on that world."[2] Similarly D.E. Jones[3] also says that his (Sweeney's) wrestling is a far cry from that of Milton's Samson and cites the following as the one possible point of contact between them:

"To live a life half dead, a living death." (Samson Agonistes)
"Death is life and life is death." (Sweeney Agonistes)

The subtitle of the play, *Fragments of an Aristophanic Melodrama,* needs further explanation. Firstly, it shows that the work is incomplete; secondly it gives the impression that it is a melodrama and thirdly it suggests an Aristophanic model. His play is 'Aristophanic' perhaps in the sense that it also combines the comic and the tragic, the crackling social satire with the plight of the Western man. It is a 'melodrama' only if the word is used in its older sense: a play that combines music and drama.[4] The onomatopoeic words, the sentence stresses, the repetitions, the songs all contribute to the creation of musical effects; to the throbbing jazz beat that syncopates the rhythms of the language of the play. Another characteristic feature of melodrama is the employment of 'flat' characters as Eliot himself argues in his essay on Ben Jonson. In this sense *Sweeney Agonistes* aptly fits the bill because all the characters in the play—with the exception of Sweeney—are 'flat'. The third characteristic feature of melodrama is the 'postponement of the *dénouement*.' "The play," asserts Carol H. Smith, "includes a postponement of the denouement in the sense that the play is a commentary on the postponement of spiritual awakening in modern man."[5] Thus, another element of melodrama, namely the requirement to drive home some kind of moral message, is also discernible in the play. Eliot's words again might help to understand the full implication of the title and subtitle and make clear what he meant to convey by them: "To those who have experienced the full horror of life, tragedy is still inadequate.... In the end horror and laughter may be one...there is potential comedy in Sophocles and potential tragedy in Aristophanes."[6]

Although D.E. Jones is not inclined "to place a strict interpretation upon the word Aristophanic," because he feels that "the resemblance to Greek Old Comedy does not go deep. The play is Aristophanic in the more general sense that it presents a satirical view of contemporary life. It is a melodrama both in the primary sense of a play, interspersed with songs and in the secondary sense of a play, in which the emotions are inflated and situations over dramatized. This inflation and the over dramatization comprise another aspect of the satire."[7] But Carol H. Smith, however, presents a slightly different interpretation to the word Aristophanic melodrama. "His play is Aristophanic in that it combines a comic surface of social satire with ritualistic celebration of death and rebirth.... Eliot's presentation is thus intended to evoke both horror and laughter in those who could see 'the potential tragedy' in Aristophanes. It is melodramatic in the older sense of the term, a play combining music and drama, because it is in the music hall tradition, but it is also melodramatic in another sense (where) there is an emphasis on plot and situation, flat characters... (and) the coincidences, resemblances and surprises of life... delaying longer than one would conceive it possible to delay, a conclusion which is inevitably and wholly foreseen"[8] and *Sweeney Agonistes* "includes a postponement of the denouement in the sense that the play is a commentary on the postponement of spiritual awakening in modern man."[9]

The epigraphs, which are always of seminal importance in Eliot and which he has placed at the beginning of the fragment, also hint at the spiritual theme of the work and secondly their arrangement also points to a likely connection between them.

Orestes: You do not see them, you don't—but I see them: they are haunting me down. I must move on—*Choephoroi.*

"Hence the soul can't be possessed of the divine union until it has divested itself of the love of the created beings."
— *St. John of the Cross.*[10]

Their arrangement points out a connection between the purgation of Orestes and of *St. John of the Cross*. The first quotation is Orestes' exit line in the *Choephoroi* when he first became aware of the Furies, who haunt and pursue him after the murder of his mother and her lover until he has achieved purgation. The passage from *St. John of the Cross* is taken from 'The Ascent of the Mount Carmel,' which describes the mystical path to the union with God. The passage is a part of the instruction to the novice who wishes to pass through the first stage of the mystical path—the dark night of the sense in which purification of all human desires must occur before the next stage is reached. In both passages purgation is the goal. Sweeney's tale of murder and the awfulness of the life-in-death existence of the murderer and others for that matter, illustrate the passage, progress and process the penitent has to undertake in order to achieve purgation. His tale is also a mundane and rather grotesque version of the epigraph of *St. John of the Cross*. According to *St. John of the Cross*, man must be purged of all human affections and desires if the distance between the creator and the creatures is to be bridged. In this argument, affections represent dependence on the senses and make demands on humans, which inevitably and irrecoverably cut them off from their first duty that is from their complete attention to God's love.

After these Epigraphs suggesting the theme of the play Eliot presents the *Fragment of a Prologue* which according to its Aristophanic prototype processes the exposition, sets the atmosphere and helps in creating a particular mood, while in the second part titled the *Fragment of Agon* he is supposed to embody a conflict, because *Agon* means conflict. Francis M. Cornford in *The Origin of Attic Comedy* explains the meaning of *Agon* as follows: "The Agon is the beginning of sacrifice in its primitive dramatic form—the conflict between the Good and the Evil principles, Summer and Winter, Life and Death. The good spirit is slain, dismembered, cooked and eaten in communal feast, and yet brought back to life."[11]

FRAGMENT OF A PROLOGUE

Dusty and Doris, the two call girls representing the degenerate soul, live in Miss. Dorrance's flat. Arnold Bennet notes in his *Journal*, "He wanted to write a drama of modern life (furnished flat sort of people) in a rhythmic prose perhaps with certain things in it accentuated by drum beats."[12] The monotonous conversation of Dusty and Doris with which the Prologue opens, the mechanical intonation of the telephone that accentuates it, and the telephonic speech of Dusty that follows it offer a good introduction to the theme of boredom.

Pereira, who is their spiritual guardian, "pays the rent"[13] and looks after their existence and well-being. Incidentally, the 'Pereira' referred to in the first section is Jonathan Pereira (1804–1853) known for his fever-reducing (!) medicine. So this Pereira is also represented as one who can cure all their ills. But Doris and Dusty cannot trust him and in their eyes, "He is no gentleman."[14] On the other hand, Sam Wauchope of the Canadian Expeditionary Force is acceptable to them. "Now Sam's a gentleman through and through."[15] The whoremonger is considered a nice boy, a funny fellow who can make you laugh. This is the glaring example of distorted value judgment of the degenerate soul.

Just then Pereira's telephone call is received which they are least inclined to respond. "The first ominous note underneath the comic surface is struck by Pereira's telephone call. (Eliot is very fond of the use of a telephone bell or doorbell or knock as an insistent signal of the entrance of divinity.)"[16] The Ting a ling a ling of Pereira's telephonic call is a "horrible noise"[17] to Doris, who doesn't talk to him and pretends to be ill. She suffers from "spiritual chill,"[18] but both she and Dusty hope that they shan't have to call a doctor. "Doris just hates having a doctor."[19] They relish the fleshiness of using mustard and water, which is a parody of fertility symbolism of resurrection.

Thus, while they avoid the curative presence of Pereira, they indulge in making false prophecy, like Madam Sosostris in *The Waste Land* by "cutting cards."[20] The first card that they cut is the "King of Clubs"[21] which they say is Pereira or "might just as well be Sweeney."[22] On another card Dusty reads "News of an absent friend"[23] who she says, might be Pereira. In *The Waste Land*, Mrs. Porter could not find "The Hanged Man." Here Dusty only gets the news of her friend who is absent. The next card is "The Queen of Hearts"[24] Mrs. Porter. Both of them alternately say about each other "Or it might be you"[25] and Doris says, "We're all hearts."[26] Thus, they are prototypes of Mrs. Porter waiting for Sweeney Apeneck. Yet they are obsessed by the unpredictability of the future events of their life. They are also afraid of "A quarrel. An estrangement. Separation of friends."[27] Doris' apprehension that the card bearing the mark of coffin prophesies her luck and symbolizes the possibility of the death of her filthy sexuality and birth of a new spiritual self. Lastly Dusty cut another card. Now it is "The Knave of Spades"[28] which she says might be "Swarts" and Doris says, "That'll be Snow."[29] This shows Doris's and Dusty's promiscuous relations with Snow and Swarts respectively. Doris's terror which has already started before the party commenced with the drawing of the two of spades that stands for the "coffin" in the pack of Tarot cards is now further intensified. The atmosphere of menace created at the beginning of the play is finally made explicit when she says, "a woman runs a terrible risk."[30] This fortune telling by cards recalls the 'Madam Sosostris' passage in the first section of *The Waste Land*.

Meanwhile, Sam Wauchope and Captain Horsfall come along with their two American friends, Mr. Klipstein and Mr. Drumpacker. They are all ex-army men who will not allow their victim to go into the shelter of Pereira. Although the tone is flippant, it is entirely fitting to the flirtatious horseplay between the men and the two women at this drinking party; the sinister undertones of seduction—if not rape and murder—are already perceivable.

Thus in this scene "the dull and almost insipid talks of Dusty and Doris, the vulgar conversation of Klipstein and Drumpacker, the telephonic conversation of Dusty and Pereira altogether exhibit Eliot's deft handling of the speech rhythm to poetic as well as dramatic purposes."[31]

FRAGMENT OF AN AGON

Here Pereira merges into Sweeney who works as the agent of purgation of Doris's degenerate soul. He is no more a frequenter to the apartment of Mrs. Porter and her daughter. On the contrary, he has become a potential spiritual force desiring to salvage the ruined creatures by enlightening them with his vision of the hollowness and vulgarities of sensual life, born of his belief in the spiritual meaning of life. His other former chums, Wauchope, Horsfall, Klipstein, Swarts and Snow for instance are removed far away from him because he has made some progress in his spiritual journey. He has overcome his sensuality and now wished to gobble up the sexual instincts of Doris. The sensual world of Doris is "a cannibal isle"[32] in which life is merely an "egg" which symbolizes procreation. Sweeney's description of the cannibal isle as a possible place to which to escape, where there are no telephones, no gramophones, no motor cars and other trappings of civilized life, but man is still governed by his pure sensual instincts and the whole span of his life has only three important events—"Birth, and Copulation and Death."[33] Doris is bored with this analysis of life. Sweeney insists on his understanding of the life lived by men around him, though he is aware of this spiritual regeneration.

On the other hand, Wauchope, Horsfall, Swarts and Snow sing the chorus of sensual enjoyment, flirtation being their "high dream"—

"Tell me in what part of the wood
Do you want to flirt with me
Under the breadfruit, banyan, palmleaf
Or under the bamboo tree?
Any old tree will do for me
Any old wood is just as good
Any old isle is just my style
Any fresh egg
Any fresh egg
And the sound of the Coral Sea"[34]

The chorus disturbs the complacency of Doris as she says:
"I don't like eggs; I never liked eggs;
And I don't like life on your crocodile isle."[35]

Now Klipstein, Drumpacker, Snow and Swarts again start their chorus of sexuality to tempt and seduce their little island girl away, where they would stay with their female counterparts for years and "wont worry what to do."[36]

"My little island girl
My little island girl
I'm going to stay with you
And we wont worry what to do."[37]

But Doris is now gradually rising above the sensual plane of life; she says in deep anguish:

"That's not life, that's no life
Why I'd just as soon be dead."[38]

Sweeney, however, emphatically says that the life she, he and others have been living is nothing but what he has already said: "Birth and copulation and death." Both Doris and Sweeney seem to have developed a sense of insufficiency.

The contrast between the new vision of Sweeney and the degenerate condition of Wauchope and others sets the Agon of the play, the struggle between the good and the evil, life and death, belief and disbelief, and the resurrection of the lost soul of Doris is in sight. Sweeney tells Doris that the real meaning of life could be visualized only after doing away with their present life of senses, because she has now fully realized that "Life is Death."[39]

Sweeney's story of the murder of a girl by a man who kept her in a bath, symbolically explains the need for the purgation of the sin of desires. "The sense of horror which Doris experiences from Sweeney's account of the murder of a girl in a bath is only an external indication of the deeper sense of sin which stirs Sweeney himself."[40] Carol H. Smith aptly remarks that "the murder and dissolution in a Lysol bath...of a girl in Sweeney's tale represents the violent murder of human desire and dissolution of the old life of birth, and copulation and death, in the sacramental purgatorial bath which will bring rebirth."[41] The story of the murder and the dissolution in a Lysol bath—a purifying as well as a killing agent—of the murdered girl represents the equally violent extinction of and watering down human desire in order to achieve salvation. The water imagery brings in connotations with birth and baptism and the dissolution of the old life succinctly summed up as:

"Birth and copulation and death
That's all the facts when you come to Brass tacks."[42]

As well as the sacramental purgatorial bath, which will bring rebirth. Or will it? For Sweeney goes on to say:

"Birth, and copulation, and death
I have been born, and once is enough
You don't remember, but I remember,
Once is enough."[43]

The repeated 'once is enough' modifies the meaning and indicates his reluctance to be reborn into a society that has been reduced to such a state. The ugliness and boredom that he sees makes him want to communicate this awareness to the other members of the party. However, his first words express only his interest in Doris and his wish to whisk her off to a cannibal isle to escape from it all:

"Sweeney: I'll carry you off
To a Cannibal isle.

Doris: You'll be the cannibal!

Sweeney: You'll be the missionary!
You'll be my seven stone Missionary!
I'll gobble you up. I'll be the cannibal.

Doris: You'll carry me off? To a Cannibal isle.

Sweeney: I'll be the cannibal.

Doris: I'll be the missionary.
I'll convert you!

Sweeney: I'll convert *you*
Into a stew
A nice little, white little, missionary Stew.

Doris: You wouldn't eat me.

Sweeney: Yes I'd eat you
In a nice little, white little, soft little
Tender Juicy little, right little missionary stew."

This curiously anticipates the death of another 'missionary,' the crucifixion of Celia in Eliot's later play *The Cocktail Party*. Here in this play also the opening exchange between Doris and Sweeney has a special ritualistic significance, which also explains the identification of Pereira with Sweeney. In the old ritual, according to Cornford, "The Doctor recalls the dead god to life, or the Cook transmutes him from age to youth. This magical process of regeneration, as we have seen, is only a special variety of death and resurrection. The Cook is a magician, a dealer in enchanted herbs, a medicine man. As such, he is not, in origin, distinct from the Learned Doctor. These two characters are alternative."[45]

Thus the theme of a spiritual pilgrimage has been very deftly woven by T.S. Eliot into the texture of a poetic play in which myth and ritual of the ancient Greece have been interwoven with hectic, artificial sensual life of the modern fashionable society. Another theme that is explored in the play is the impossibility or difficulty of communication, a very Beckett-like concern. A sense of spiritual isolation, which is associated with all Eliot's protagonists is vaguely suggested in Sweeney's problem of communication also:

"Sweeney: I gotta use words when I talk to you
　　　　　But if you understand or if you don't
　　　　　That's nothing to me and nothing to you
　　　　　We all gotta do what we gotta do
　　　　　We're gona sit here and drink this booze
　　　　　We're gona sit here and have a tune
　　　　　We're gona stay and we're gona go
　　　　　And somebody gotta pay the rent."[46]

Then finally while the transformation is taking place, the slow crescendo of the knocks heralds the arrival of the dangerous Pereira, the hangman. The 'finale' of the chorus provides the link between Sweeney's story and that of the various members of the party. It is the communal yet marvelously colloquial expression of terror and fear. The nightmare-like expression of the terror and fear of what is coming to all of us is accentuated by the relentless pursuit of the hoo-ha's of the chorus. This is the modern version of the 'Hound of Heaven' theme where the Furies will not only haunt us but will also hunt us down to mete out our punishment.

The function of the play's all pervasive rhythm gains further significance here. On the one hand, the ominous pounding rhythm contributes to sustaining and intensifying the looming menace of the hunt and audibly re-enacts the chase where the pursuing feet are closing in on the prey. "The final song sung by the 'full chorus' is a description of the nightmare like pursuit of the penitent by the purgatorial forces. As the epigraph from Aeschylus suggests, the hoo-ha's serve the same function as the relentless Furies in their pursuit of Orestes. This is Eliot's version of the 'Hound of Heaven' theme."[47]

"And you wait for the knock and the turning of a lock
For you know the hangman's waiting for you
And perhaps you are alive
And perhaps you are dead
Hoo ha ha
Hoo ha ha
Hoo
Hoo
Hoo
Knock Knock Knock
Knock Knock Knock
Knock
Knock
Knock"[48]

In this way *Sweeney Agonistes* is Eliot's first experiment in the field of drama. He has tried to fuse the ancient and the modern together to present a powerful piece of dramatic art. Dealing with the eternal theme of the Senses and the Spirit, between Life and Death and between Light and Darkness, he has presented three groups of characters in *Sweeney Agonistes*. There is a group of characters like Wauchope, Horsfall, Klipstein, Drumpacker, Snow and Swarts, who rejoice only in their physical, sensual existence and try to elude the uninitiated soul of Doris away from her guide, the saviour and the redeemer Pereira or it may be Sweeney, who form the other group. Both these forces, the sensual and spiritual try to pull Doris in different directions but ultimately she realizes the nightmarish dream at the end of the play. Amidst the melodramatic hoo-ha of the chorus she hears the knock at the door and Sweeney's message that Life is Death and Death is Life, is understood by Doris. She now feels bored of 'Birth, and Copulation and Death' and seems fully prepared for Death, the Second Birth, the realization of the immortality of the soul.

The different levels of human life as depicted in Eliot's plays also depict the different levels along which the plays move. D.E. Jones says that these levels of his plays reproduce "the different levels—sensuous, logical, psychological and spiritual—upon which life is lived."[49] This led Eliot to conceive his theory of dramatic levels providing a theatre with "something for everybody."[50] The dramatic formula which he evolved at this early stage of his dramatic career included various planes of meaning to match the different planes of understanding of the audience. T.S. Eliot has himself described this in *The Use of Poetry and the Use of Criticism:*

> "The most useful poetry, socially, would be one which could cut across all the present stratifications of public taste—stratification which are perhaps a sign of social disintegration.... For the simplest auditors there is the plot, for the most thoughtful the character and conflict of character, for the more literary the words and phrasing, for the more musically sensitive the rhythm, and for the auditors of greater sensitiveness and understanding a meaning which reveals itself gradually.... My intention was to have one character whose sensibility and intelligence should be on the plane of the most sensitive and intelligent members of the audience; his speeches should be addressed to them as much as to the other personages in the play—or rather, should be addressed to the latter who were to be material, literal-minded and visionless, with the consciousness of being overheard by the former. There was to be an understanding between the protagonist and a small number of the audience, while the rest of the audience, would share the responses of other characters of the play. Perhaps this is all too deliberate, but one must experiment as one can."[51]

This very idea has been very aptly summed up by M.C. Bradbrook when he says, "He wrote with the idea that the spectators, like the characters, would be graded in degrees of understanding, that only a few would understand the hero. For the rest, since he hoped for a popular audience, he depended on doing monkey tricks behind the audience's back."[52]

In this way "the treatment of the characters in *Sweeney Agonistes* conforms to Eliot's idea of stylized surface. They are undeniably 'flat,' and with the possible exception of Sweeney, are sketched in the broad outline of intentional caricature. Doris and Dusty (a name suggestive of *The Waste Land* imagery) are lower class prostitutes. They are both superstitious and superficial and are differentiated only by Sweeney's more sustained attention to Doris."[53]

Sweeney is by far the most important and interesting character in the play. "He introduces the dimension of tragic horror into the world of Dusty and Doris and others. In the character of Sweeney some of the ritual elements which Eliot incorporated into the play from the work of Cornford and his Cambridge colleagues become apparent. Eliot's intention, I believe, was to make Sweeney an ironical buffoon-hero in Cornford sense. The hero of the comedy had his wisdom in feigned stupidity, which was a mask for cunning and slyness."[54] "Whatever elements of parody appear in the fragments, Eliot's purpose is to present a picture of the tragic aspects of urban life caught in the rhythms of the jazz."[55]

"Sweeney's spiritual awakening has set him apart from the rest of the cast of the poem. He is speaking to them, but his words communicate no meaning to them. It is because his experience of life is not theirs, because his belief is not shared by them, because they are still in their infernal world of senses. Moreover, spiritual insight cannot be thrust into the mind of others. It is a personal achievement of a man of belief, who experiences the travails of life and transcends its surface and is ready "to pay the rent" of the house he is living in, that is his body by sacrificing his physical self.

"In the end all the degenerate men are wrapped in the halo of Sweeney's insight. Their chorus explains the nightmarish condition of the mystic journey undertaken by a penitent, the lonely journey in the middle of the dark night of the soul when purgatorial forces visit him. He waits for the knock of the "hangman" (i.e. the Hanged Man of *The Waste Land*) who would open the lock of the dark room of his ignorance and lechery and redeem his soul. Only then perhaps, he will be really 'alive' although his former physical self would be dead. Thus the poem which began with the portrayal of the *Inferno* and opened its canvas of the *Purgatorio* closes at the door of *Paradiso*."[56]

Eliot, thus, combines in *Sweeney Agonistes,* the technique of Greek comedy with Jazz music of the 20th century. In doing so, he has adopted the Aristophanic model of comedy with its Prologue, the Agon, and the Parabasis (in which the chorus comes forward and speaks directly to the audience). He has revived the chorus on the Aeschylean model, where the chorus and the Histrionic elements are held in a balance and fused into an organic whole. The chorus forms an inseparable part of the play and helps in advancing the action of the play.

In *Sweeney Agonistes* the chorus is sung at three different places. While parodying the Shakespearean lyric of the play *As You Like It,* Eliot transforms the song 'Under the Greenwood Tree' into a parody: 'Under the Bamboo Tree,' where the parody itself becomes the reality. The chorus, here, is the chorus of sexuality, but Doris who seems completely bored of sensual life, gradually prepares herself for her Death. Even Snow and Swarts get interested in Sweeney's story of the girl who was done in. Sweeney, the cannibal, finally converts Doris into "a nice little, white little, missionary stew." But purgation is not yet complete unless Sweeney gobbles up the stew or does the girl in. But then finally the Agon culminates into a melodramatic close when the full chorus presents a nightmare depicting the knocking of the fate at the door of the penitent. "The fear of the Unknown has been beautifully depicted in the melodramatic Hoo-Ha of the concluding chorus"[57] spoken as *Parabasis.*

"It is significant that the final song is sung by the 'full chorus'.... The chorus takes one side, then the other, and finally is won over to the side of the virtue represented by the hero. In *Sweeney Agonistes* the chorus in the beginning of the Agon indicates its endorsement of the copulation theme, but in the end it too voices the final purgatorial ode."[58]

In fact, *Sweeney Agonistes* anticipates Eliot's later plays in its skilful adaptation of modern speech rhyme in dramatic dialogue and in its clever use into the choric form. Its great achievement was to show how the use of the chorus made drama more powerful and with this aim in view he initiated the chorus in *Sweeney Agonistes*. It has been beautifully woven into the texture of its theme and the plot plays a positive role in depicting the conflict and the dénouement. In the beginning "the chorus expresses its agreement with the 'copulation theme' but at the end endorses the substance of the final 'Purgatorial Ode.'"[59] As Cornford in *The Origin of Attic Comedy* says, "In Aristophanes, the opponents attempt, in Agon, to woo the sympathies of the chorus, which initially takes one side and then the other and is finally won over to the side represented by the hero."[60] This convention of the Old Comedy of Aristophanes has been faithfully adopted by Eliot.

In the field of language also *Sweeney Agonistes* provides some clues to analyse Eliot's experiments towards the creation of a new dramatic language. Here "Eliot's chief concern was to come to terms with the speech of the time."[61] Using chorus to voice the communal feelings, he also uses the language of the common man. "Besides incorporating the incantatory rhythms of the Jazz songs and the conversational tones of the telephonic dialogues, Eliot has introduced another aural device into the diction of the play. Such a device, according to Grover Smith exemplified the playwright's recourse to 'music hall style.' It implies a kind of bouncing of a line from one speaker to another. What is important is the repeated use of the same word, meant to extract greater attention, appeal and emphasis. The latter part of the *Fragment of Prologue* abounds in such aural effects of the dramatic language."[62] But the most typical example of this effect which Eliot has achieved through the use of repeated sound is to be found at the end of the *Fragment of Agon*, when the chorus speaks out the Parabasis with its Hoo-Haa and Knocks, with a view to contributing to the rhythmic cadence of the play.

However, it is also in its incorporation of the contemporary diction and idiom into the drama that *Sweeney Agonistes* occupies a significant place in the scheme of Eliot's dramatic art. Its dramatic verse, irrespective of the presence of the symbol and myths, shows the promise of a modern vocabulary. Eliot's experiment to develop a suitable language for the drama of his age is in perfect harmony with his dramatic theory. In the *Sacred Wood*, he quotes Aristotle, "Novices in the art attain to finish off diction and precision of portraiture before they can construct the plot."[63] *Sweeney Agonistes*, therefore, presents the model of a suitable diction without the least effort to construct plot.

"Eliot has also incorporated into the play the popular songs of the Jazz era. These songs present such a close imitation of contemporary Jazz music that parody becomes the things parodied," for example:

"Under the bamboo tree
Two live as one
One live as two
Two live as three
Under the bam
Under the boo
Under the bamboo tree."[64]

"This is based on a song by Bob Cole and J. Rosamond Johnson, first published in London in 1905. Eliot's tune is different, but he has borrowed from the original song, the title and the last two lines of his Chorus."[65]

"It is really revealing to mention how Eliot discards the conventional metres of the drama in favour of Jazz rhythms in *Sweeney Agonistes*. The choice indicated the way he wanted to recreate a new metrical form suitable to drama. Realising that rhythm formed an important element in the art of Shakespeare, Charlie Chaplin, Massine and the juggling Rastelli, it was natural for Eliot to think that rhythmic beauty must be brought back to the dramatic language. Equally significant is Eliot's contention that a man who devises 'new rhythms' is one who extends and refines our sensibility...." Eliot states that the conditions of modern life have altered our 'perception of rhythms,' hence the rejections of the conventional tones by him in *Sweeney Agonistes*, is more than a technical matter. It involves a specific principle and a theory.

The choice of Jazz rhythms for the play displays a clear device to match the Jazz surface of the contemporary atmosphere. How minutely does Eliot realize the rhythms of primitive and modern metrics, is evident from his instruction to Hallie Flanagan who staged *Sweeney Agonistes* at Vassar in 1933. "I had intended the whole play," says Eliot "to be accompanied by the light drum taps to accentuate the beats, especially the chorus which ought to have a noise like a street drill."[66]

Thus we find that in *Sweeney Agonistes* "the poet has injected into his music hall rhythms, the full force of an intense spiritual experience, so the silly songs frequently become a ritual formulae charged with philosophical or religious allusions. It is again the Metaphysical's way of joining together the trivial and the serious."[67]

Thus as Raymond William says that in *Sweeney Agonistes*, "a form is discovered, not so much in characters and action, and not in any conclusive way in a pattern of experience, but rather in an inclusive ordering of speech. It is in the success of rhythms like these that *Sweeney Agonistes* marks such a notable advance."[68] "*Sweeney,* then is drama only in intention; but in fact it is poetry, and significant poetry, containing the seeds of much of Eliot's later work."[69]

Thus we can safely call *Sweeney Agonistes* as a Prelude to Eliot's great experiment in the field of drama wherein he has experimented with the potentials of the great Attic Drama, without losing any sight of the contemporary world. M.C. Bradbrook has rightly said, "*Sweeney Agonistes*, though but a fragment, is perhaps his most modern play."[70] In *Sweeney Agonistes* we can find virtually all of Eliot's major dramatic ideas that he meticulously explored in his numerous essays: a chorus, an accentuated rhythm, attic sources, the use of myth along with music-hall turns, colloquial speech patterns and an underlining Jazz beat. The play heralds a new epoch in the field of drama with its novel use of the chorus, which gives his poetic plays a new dimension.

(B) *THE ROCK*

Eliot's next excursion into drama was *The Rock*, a pageant play written in aid of a church building fund and aptly taking the building of a church as its framework. It was presented in the spring of 1934, on behalf of the Forty-Five Churches Fund of the Diocese of London as a plea for Church building. Here Eliot was writing under the direction of E. Martin Browne who wrote the scenario. In his Prefatory Note to the play, Eliot has disclaimed the authorship of all but the Choruses and one scene presumably the last scene in Part I—the one scene entirely in verse, although the printed version of the play announces that the entire book of words is by T.S. Eliot. However, Eliot writes in his prefatory note:

> "I cannot consider myself the author of the play, but only of words which are printed here. The scenario incorporating some historical scenes suggested by Rev. Webb-Odell, is by Mr. E. Martin Browne, under whose direction I wrote the choruses and dialogues, and submissive to whose expert direction I rewrote much of them. Of only one scene am I literally the author; for this scene and for the sentiments expressed in the choruses I must assume the responsibility."[1]

Eliot has therefore chosen to preserve only the choruses and they are reprinted in the *Collected Poems*. Eliot provided the verse choruses, and some of the prose dialogues for a prepared scenario, telling of the development of the Christian Church, linking this to work on an actual church building in contemporary London in 1934. Much of the verse is deeply grounded in the Bible—in its language, imagery and rhythm. The play makes no pretence of being a contribution to English dramatic literature. It is not quite accurate to call *The Rock* a play. It is a pageant not a real drama, for there is no central conflict or intense struggle in it. It is merely a series of scenes, which illustrate the founding of the Church and all the tribulations that have fortified it and the final triumph of the Church. The chorus is most significant thing about *The Rock*. The chorus assuming a Greek role of commentary also provides the piece with musical richness. The verse of the choruses with their metrical diversity anticipate the still more beautiful choric speeches in *The Murder in the Cathedral.*

Eliot himself called *The Rock* a "revue" and E. Martin Browne who directed the production at Sadler's Well, has elaborated on Eliot's term: "A pageant was called for, to promote the building of churches in Greater London.... After many months in which we found ourselves equally puzzled by the problem of how to create an interesting form, while retaining what the pageant-elements demanded, we agreed on a scenario, based on the structure of the type of 'revue' then current under the aegis of Charles Cochram: the difference being that instead of Young Ladies relying on their physical charms, (they together with their male counterparts) wore half masks and garments of stiff hessian and relied on the application of their vocal agility to Mr. Eliot's verse."[2] The necessity was to communicate with an audience, which would, if reached by *The Rock's* message, respond with generous contribution to the Forty-Five Churches Fund.

This became *The Rock*, the choruses of which described London and its suburbs as the busy center of a desolating, meaningless, commercial activity. "It is a clearer, more sermon-like picture of the life-in-death of *The Waste Land* and *Sweeney Agonistes*; and now, for the first time is added the sharp declaration of Christian faith by which hope and meaning are given to the endless cycles of time, which without this hope and meaning 'bring us farther from God and nearer to the dust.'"[3]

In suggesting the title to this work "Eliot is drawing upon the Biblical use of the word *'Rock.'* In Psalms, David is thus represented as supplicating God: 'Thou art my father, my God/ and the rock of my salvation' (LXXXIV, 26). Again the image of a church to be built on a rock occurs in the words of Christ to Peter: 'Thou art Peter, and upon this rock I will build my church' (Matthew xvi, 18). The word *'Rock'* in these contexts signifies God in his aspect of supporting strength for weak mankind. Indeed, much of the verse is deeply grounded in the Bible, in respect of language, imagery, rhythm and symbolism."[4]

So, besides all this biblical perspective, for a proper understanding of the play some knowledge of the pageant is also necessary, but since it is no longer in print, an account of the action may be somewhat useful. Drawing mainly from D.E. Jones' analysis of the action of *The Rock*,[5] it is found that the action opens with the building of a church in contemporary London; it begins by emphasising that the building of the church is not a matter of merely piling up stones. It ranges back and forth in time to show the continuity of ecclesiastical tradition, the persistence of the past into the present, and the way in which present is built upon the past. This new church is built upon *The Rock* (Matthew xvi, 18). The chorus of seven men and ten women, wearing half-masks to emphasise their impersonality, speak as the voice of the church and the 'Rock' himself is one of the *Dramatic Personae*.

In the Opening, chorus, the spiritual sickness of contemporary society, is diagnosed as the "knowledge of words and ignorance of the Word"[6]; as a result of which we are simply moving "farther from God and nearer to dust."[7] Then the Rock enters the scene led by a Boy and exhorts the audience:

"I say to you: Make perfect your will
I say: take no thought of the harvest,
But only of proper sowing."[8]

Then he invites us to see 'the work of the humble'[9] and this introduces the choruses contrasting the work of the men building churches with the plight of the unemployed. Eventually our attention is focused upon a small group of workmen who are 'discovered' digging and building the foundations of a church. Most of them are indifferent about the building they are working on. To them it is just another job. But Ethelbert, the foreman, is alive to its significance, and the workmen then chant about building a Church together. They chant about the need for building and having a job for everyone:

A Church for all
And a job for each
Each man to his work.[10]

"The chorus itself, as in classical Greek drama, is primarily there to provide a commentary on the action, and speaks in the first person. The biblical language, with many images and phrases and cadences drawn from the Bible, is fundamental to the whole of *The Rock,* but it is mixed with ordinary colloquial speech to give an up-to-date yet timeless feel to the verse."[11] The talk among the workers is in their typically stunted idiom, providing a caricature of working class speech, for which Eliot himself may not be responsible. Shortly after this conversation, a group of Saxons enter the stage.

Through the *Second Chorus* the workmen witness the acceptance of Christianity in Britain, the foundation of the English Church:

Thus your fathers were made

Fellow citizens of the saints, of the household of God, being built upon the foundation

Of apostles and prophets, Christ Jesus Himself the Chief cornerstone.[12]

Thus the building of the Church is not an isolated act. It is a part of the larger process of founding and maintaining the Church temporal. The difficulties of building the church in this sense are perennial—"The Church must be forever building, for it is forever decaying within and attacked from without;"[13] so there is:

Much to cast down, much to build, much to restore;
Let the work not delay, time and the arm not waste:[14]

"The long sentences in this Chorus are closer to prose than poetry: the feeling is that we are listening to the exhortations of a sermon.... There is also a notable to-and-fro movement between different tenses. For example, the past of history in the opening phrase 'Thus your fathers were,' is contrasted with the present situation of 'you now sit helpless' by the end of the sentence.... These shifts mirror the sense of the Church being forever built in the past and decaying in the present, and needing rebuilding in the future."[15]

The *Third Chorus*, then reflects upon the unfortunate life of crafty godless creatures—"the wretched generation of enlightened men,"[16] whom Eliot has beautifully described as "decent godless people whose monuments are the asphalt road/ And a thousand lost golf balls."[17] God's home is beautiful, His sanctuary is peaceful, which will not be found in life deprived of spiritual realization. If we forget the way to the Temple we will never get peace and ultimately face Death, who will never forget to come to the door.

"Though you forget the way to the Temple,
There is one who remembers the way to your door:
Life you may evade, but Death you shall not."[18]

"This chorus is an imitation of the way the prophets in the Bible bring 'the Word of the Lord' to an erring people, and is appropriately full of biblical echoes. Particularly striking are the emphatic questions...and emphatic repetitions throughout.... These plentiful incantatory repetitions add to the questions in giving urgency as well as emphasis to the poetic and prophetic utterance of this whole Chorus."[19]

The Fourth Chorus then points to the difficulties that the builders of the church have to face:

"There were enemies without to destroy him,

And spies and self-seekers within,

When he and his men laid their hands to rebuilding the wall"[20]

So we must build "with sword in one hand and the trowel in the other"[21]

The Fifth Chorus also repeats the same idea and warns us that "We are encompassed with snakes and dogs; therefore some must labour, and others must hold the spears."[22]

Finally the theme of the temporal forces at war with the church is presented in *The Rock* in a way, which anticipates *Murder in the Cathedral*. *The Sixth Chorus* asserts that:

"...Son of Man was not crucified once for all,
The blood of the martyrs not shed once for all,
The lives of Saints not given once for all:
But the Son of Man is crucified always."[23]

and that "if blood of martyrs is to flow on the steps/ We must first build the steps."[24] It is with this spirit that we must built the temple. "The act of building of the Church must continue through the re-enactment of the Sacrifice of Christ by the Saints

Sweeney Agonistes and Other Fragments 63

and the martyrs.... This urgent call to martyrdom given by the Chorus may serve as the befitting prologue to Eliot's plays which dramatise the theme of martyrdom in their ritual underpattern."[25]

"Then in a scene reminiscent of German Expressionism and very like the kind of drama younger poets of the time, notably Auden and Spender were attempting—in the only scene which is entirely in verse—squads of Redshirts and Blackshirts enter in military formation and offer their solutions to the problems of contemporary society."[26]

Redshirts (in unison with military gestures).

Our verse
is free
as the wind on the steppes
as love in the heart of the factory worker
thousands and thousands of steppes
millions and millions of workers
all working
all loving
in the cities
on the steppes
production has risen by twenty point
six per cent
we can laugh at God!
our workers
all working
our turbines
all turning
our sparrows
all chirping
all denounce you, deceivers of the people!

(The parody of free verse and the parody of communist claims—free love, increasing production, the sparrows backing up the workers in denunciation, go together.)

Blackshirts (saluting). Hail!
We come as a bon and a blessing to all,
Though we'd rather appear in the Albert Hall

Our methods are new in this land of the free,
We make the deaf hear and we make the blind see.
We are law-keeping fellows who make our own laws—
And we welcome *Subscriptions in Aid of the Cause*!

Just while this goes on, the rock is revealed 'standing brooding on the pinnacle':

The Rock
There shall be always the Church and the World
And the Heart of Man
Shivering and fluttering between the,
        choosing and chosen,
Valiant, ignoble, dark and full of light
Swinging between Hell Gate
        and Heaven gate
And the Gates of Hell shall not prevail.
Darkness now, then
Light.
Light.[27]

Part II neatly takes up the theme by going back to time before there was light. Presumably this Part began in darkness and light came up on cue; as *The Seventh Chorus* says:

In the beginning *God* created the world,
Waste and void, Waste and void.
And darkness was upon the face of the deep.[28]

The chorus rapidly surveys the history of the world to the time of Christ, the coming of light of revelation and the foundation of the Church. It also calls upon us to realize the supreme importance of martyrdom, which enacts the Passion and Sacrifice of Christ. Eliot has beautifully described the meaning, importance and significance of Incarnation. He says:

"Then came at a predetermined moment, a moment in time and of time,
A moment not out of time, but in time, in what we call history:
Transecting, bisecting the world of time, a moment in time but not like a moment of time.

A Moment in time but time was made through that moment:
for without the meaning there is no time,
and that moment of time gave the meaning."[29]

"But in our age something has happened that has never happened before."[30] Men have forsaken spiritual values and have disowned the church.

"So we today—
But stand with empty hands and; alms turned upwards
In an age which advances progressively backwards?"[31]

And to the Chorus finally questions:

"Has the Church failed mankind or has mankind failed the Church?"[32]

"A vast stretch of history is here compressed into four paragraphs before the fragments of speech of the unemployed and the final questions and comments of the chorus. The first paragraph deals with the Creation, with appropriate quotations from the Genesis; the next presents the 'Higher Religions,' which led men to the light but came to 'a dead end'; then there is Christ, the one accepted way to come to the light; and the fourth paragraph lambasts the atheism of the present age, which 'advances progressively backwards.' In the first three paragraphs there is the repeated assertion of light leading to light, but 'light' is significantly absent from the modern age, which has only the 'darkness on the face of the deep.' This biblical quotation appears, joined with repetition of another phrase with a biblical echo, 'Waste and void' in each section except the one devoted to Christ, to underline the difference between the truly enlightened Christian way and both the earlier strivings towards the light and the benighted state of the present that the chorus bewails."[33]

"But the Church is still there to remind men of the truth. The Rock sends 'one who accomplished much, in a time of drought and desolation/ Blomfield, Bishop of London,/ Builder of many churches' and thus the action of Part II is initiated. Bishop Blomfield tells the chorus that conditions were no more favourable to the building of churches in his own time and suggests they take as example from the Crusades, which were set in motion 'by a few men of principles and conviction,' such as 'can accomplish what men without principles and conviction deem impossible.'"[34] *The Eighth Chorus* boldly asserts:

> Yet nothing is impossible, nothing,
> To men of faith and conviction.
> Let us therefore make perfect our will.
> O God, help us.[35]

"The scenes thus introduced serve to bring a touch of chivalric colour and give an opportunity for the introduction of liturgical poem. The action (then) digresses even further from the central theme. A visit to the sight by Mrs. Ethelbert serves as an excuse for a toast to the church and a song by her and Ethelbert. A visit by some members of the 'upper class' gives rise to a discussion of styles of church architecture and leads to a scene of 'Reformation times' in which Romish decoration is stripped from the churches. This in turn gives rise to a fine Chorus"[36]: *The Ninth Chorus* exhorts to the audience:

> Son of Man, behold with thine eyes, and hear with thine ears
> And set thine heart upon all that I show thee.[37]

The Chorus also reminds us that the House of God is the House of Sorrow, because it reminds us of the Sacrifice of Christ. So we must devote our life—the spirit and the body—to the building of the Temple of God. "Eliot here extends the previous dichotomy of Nature and God, Time and Eternity, to cover also his old preoccupation with flesh and spirit in humanity"[38]:

> For Man is joined spirit and body,
> And therefore must serve as spirit and body
> Visible and invisible, two worlds meet in Man
> Visible and invisible must meet in His Temple;
> You must not deny the body.[39]

The House of God, where on the altar there will be the Crucifix and the Light, which will be the symbol of the Invisible Light of God. The completion of the Church of Ethelbert and his men is in sight:

Now you shall see the Temple completed;
After much striving, after many obstacles;
For the work of creation is never without travail;
The formed stone, the visible crucifix,
The dressed altar, the lifting light,
Light
Light
The visible reminder of Invisible Light.[40]

"Then there follows a dramatization of the legendary dedication of Westminster Abbey by St. Peter, the Rock on which the Church was founded. The play returns splendidly to the theme, but the next moment it is off again, this time into a ballet on the legend of Dick Wittington and his cat, justified flimsily as a transition to the dedication of the rebuilt Church of St. Michael, Paternoster Royal. A conversation piece between Wren, Pepys and Evelyn leads to the dedication of St. Paul's and *The Final Chorus* is spoken around the alter of the new Church 'now furnished and lighted.'"[41]

It is now a visible church, one more light set on a hill

In a world confused and dark and disturbed by portents of fear.[42]

But Eliot also cautions us of the Devil who always lies in ambush to devour the innocent and the week that must seek faith in the light of God:

The great snake lies ever half awake, at the bottom of the pit of the world, curled.[43]

And finally concludes with a hymn of thanks—giving to the 'Light Invisible' for inspiring us to search the light of belief to dispel the Darkness of Despair from our hearts:

O Light Invisible, We give Thee thanks for Thy great glory![44]

Then finally with a short speech by the Rock 'now St. Peter' the benediction and communal singing of the Builders' song, the pageant ends. It is the final chorus that is best of all the utterances of *The Rock*. This passage with rich lyric splendour describes the light of the Church, a city set on a hill shining against the darkness. The chorus sings in praise of "Light

Invisible." Thus the pageant ends in a ritual of prayer that sweeps the audience into an act of worship. It was written for a Christian audience on a Christian occasion.

"In the light imagery of this concluding Chorus, the poet is not only using traditional biblical associations but imitating Dante in the final Canto of *Paradise,* of which Eliot remarked: 'Nowhere in poetry has experience so remote from ordinary experience been expressed so concretely, by a masterly use of that imagery of *light* which is the form of certain types of mystical experience.' By his imitation, Eliot also uses concrete visual images of a large range of types of light to suggest the spiritual, Invisible Light. Every part of this Chorus has reference to light, building to a climax: the first paragraph has the church as a light on a hill, the next the light of guidance for the believer, and then the great accumulation of lesser lights is brilliantly made to slow down and 'tire' at human tiring of light before the verse gathers momentum again towards the final ecstatic gratefulness. It concludes *Selected Poems* on a note of spiritual upliftment that is worlds away from the despair and disillusion of the earlier part of the volume."[45]

Carol H. Smith has very briefly and beautifully summarized the action of *The Rock:* Its scenes depict the efforts and difficulties of a group of London masons involved in building a church. The difficulties they encounter, intended to suggest the obstacles faced by the church in the modern world, include bad foundations, lack of money, the hostility of agitators, and hostile criticism from secular groups represented by the *Blackshirts,* the *Redshirts* and the *Plutocrats.* The process of construction is seen at every stage from the setting of the foundation to the finishing of the church in preparation for dedication.

"Interspersed among the scenes showing the actions of the modern church builders are a series of pageant scenes from the past, showing related situations in the history of the Church, including the conversion of King Sabert by Melletus, Rahere's building of St. Bartholomew's, the rebuilding of Jerusalem, the Danish Invasion, the dedication of Westminster Abbey, outburst of Puritan iconoclasm, and a conversation between Wren, Pepys and Evelyn. The hooded figure of *The Rock* representing the Church as eternal witness, sufferer and martyr, in contrast to the chorus which represents the Church in action, is intended to serve the dramatic function of supporting the chorus by putting its commentary on the events witnessed in the framework of the eternal and ever continuing struggles of the Church"[46]

Connected with the Christian conception of action and suffering is the theme of the interaction of time and eternity in the experience of religious awareness. The Rock expresses the idea, which becomes one of Eliot's favourite dramatic utterances in this manner:

Remember, all you who are numbered for God,
In every moment of time you live where two worlds cross,
In every moment you live at a point of intersection,
Remember, living in time, you must live also now in Eternity.

"The point of intersection is also identified with the divine point, which moves the wheel of time, 'the still point in the turning wheel.' The wheel image first used in the opening chorus has been used by Eliot in both his dramatic and non-dramatic poetry. The still point which turns the moving wheel is both the recognition of God possible at every moment and in history, the moment of the Incarnation."[47] "This motif, crucial to the pageant, is expressed in the dualism of chorus and *The Rock*, of present and past workmen, and in the symbols of change and eternity."[48]

According to Carol H. Smith, through the chorus and the figure of the Rock, very likely, "Eliot initially conceived the work to be a new exemplification of his theory of dramatic levels. The prose scenes, representing the actions of the modern day builders, were to be the surface of the drama, which has to be given an added dimension of historical and cultural importance by the insertion of relevant incidents from the past, one of Eliot's favourite methods of conveying simultaneous analogy and irony. The stereotype character conceptions might have seemed, in scenario, to fit very well his conceptions of flat humour characters used to achieve a stylized surface which would not interfere with the symbolic level beneath the action."[49]

Commenting on the absence of the dramatic conflict on one side and the profuseness of meditative poetry of the chorus on the other, F.O. Matthiessen says: "*The Rock* is a pageant, not a drama. That is to say, its situation does not give rise to any intense struggle or conflict; its structure consists of a series of scenes of a related tone, scenes which decorate the theme of building of the Church, the hardships it has encountered in various crises of the past as well as the present, and the firmness of its triumph."[50]

The dramatic deficiencies of *The Rock* arise from the fact that the situation does not give rise to any intense struggle or conflict, its structure consists merely of a series of scenes which do not evince any dramatic development of anything like a plot. It also failed to come up to Eliot's idea of a verse play.

"The scenario was not written by Eliot, but was provided by E. Martin Browne. Eliot's task was simply to produce the dialogues, the bulk of which is in prose. Many of the scenes are hardly of any dramatic interest. Their original purpose was to furnish a formal spectacle, which was accompanied by music and ballet." But the passages in verse which run to several hundred lines, though spoken mostly by the chorus, also include the whole of the most energetic scene in which the chorus is confronted by Redshirts, Blackshirts and Plutocrats.[51] This scene shows Eliot trying his hand at the kind of material, which Auden later experimented in *the Dance of Death*.

The chorus Leader introduces the Rock, as "The Witness, The Critic, The Stranger, and The God-shaken in whom is the truth inborn." He appears to be the presiding spirit of the whole pageant, who advises men to make perfect their will, and reminds them of the eternal moral problem of the struggle of good and evil. His philosophical utterances are almost echoed by the chorus, and his final emergence as St. Peter only explains the meaning of his symbolic presence in the play. Nevertheless, as the protagonist of the play he represents the eternal aspect of the Church Spiritual which emerges through the actions of the

Martyrs and Saints. Other characters of the play, Alfred, Ethelbert, Edwin, the Blackshirts and Redshirts are like flitting shadows: they do not receive any individuality. They just voice the ideas of the playwright—like the voice of the poet speaking to others.[52] As Eliot himself says in *The Three Voices of Poetry* "This chorus of *The Rock* was not a dramatic voice; though many lines were distributed, the personages were unindividuated. Its members were speaking *for me*, not uttering words that really represented any supposed character of their own."[53]

The choruses of *The Rock* "give voice to some of the most profound kind of meditative poetry that he was to develop later in his *Quartets;* although it hardly meets Eliot's test for a religious play 'that should be able to hold the interest, to arouse the excitement of people who are not religious, nor through the very nature of its inception could it possibly rise to his far more exacting demand of creating an indisseverable double pattern of poetry and drama."[54]

"Working to a scenario, he was mainly concerned, in writing the choruses, to provide links between the scenes. In this task there was nothing to stimulate a truly dramatic conception, to call forth what he calls the third or dramatic voice. Consequently, it was the second voice—that of himself, 'addressing—indeed haranguing—an audience,' as he puts it 'that was most distinctly audible.' The members of the chorus were not individualized; they had no character of their own. They merely served as a voice-piece for the author's views."[55]

The Rock, thus does not realize the unifying conception latent in it. There is no dramatic emotion in the choruses to fuse the parts. They simply reflect different poetic moods; occasionally a devotional mood, but more often an elegiac mood of mourning for the wholeness of the vision now lost to the society, or a satiric mood in which the superficiality of modern life is castigated.

"As it is much of the later part is just scene spinning. One can almost hear the authors asking themselves, what can we do next to give variety? The pageant becomes a sort of extravaganza on the building of Churches instead of the dramatic meditation on the building of the Church adumbrated in the opening scenes."[56]

Commenting on the functions of the chorus in *The Rock*, Carol H. Smith says: "The chorus was to serve both as the vehicle of social commentary in the Greek sense and a dramatic instrument for piercing through the level of surface action to the level of philosophical and theological implications of the action. Since Eliot was convinced that philosophical ideas must be translated into emotions before being presented in poetry, the task of the chorus was to present the ideological commentary on the action in a poetic form which would make the audience feel, as well as understand, the more profound implications of the events."[57] This new use of the chorus marked a move in the direction of a more integrated relationship between the levels and at the same time towards more direct communication with the audience.

The choruses of *The Rock* are also significant as a stage in the creation of a new verse form. Martin Browne explains this accomplishment saying that, a contemporary speech rhythm is essential, and two developments follow. First, the iambic foot of Shakespearean tradition is given up: the stress shifts to the beginning of the foot, in accordance with the change that has come over English speech. This trochaic-cum-dactylic foot is of course no more rigidly adhered to than was the iambic in Shakespeare's later plays. The verse is infinitely varied, with many inverted feet; but rhythm is strongly maintained.

"The other change is a final freeing of the verse from the counting of syllables. The ten-syllable line of 'blank verse', which was almost uniform in Shakespeare's early plays, came to vary from eight to fourteen syllables in his later ones: but still the ten-syllable basis was at the back of the minds of both writer and hearers. Eliot has broken this blank verse tradition of syllables by going at once back and forward. He has gone back to the basis established by the medieval poets, of a fixed number of *Stresses* in the line without any fixed number of syllables. He has gone forward to meet the development of prose rhythms by the inclusion of a very long, sweepingly rhythmic line having six or eight stresses, but still a part of the verse structure. Thus a form of verse much more varied that any before was placed at the service of the theatre."[58] Thus the choric verse in *The Rock* shows a great metrical diversity. Musically, these Choruses rank among Eliot's best poems.[59]

Apart from this significant experiment in the verse form of the choruses there is also a great variety of verse used in the pageant. Grover Smith has admirably summed them up as, "The verse of the pageant is of seven or eight different types. One of these occurs uniquely in the Kiplingesque comic song sung by Ethelbert; this has a Savoyard or music hall flavour like other light verse of Eliot. Another occurs in the 'Builders' Song' (presumably indebted to Blake), which sporadically interpolates into the action a reminder of the central theme, the contemporary need for the building of the churches. A third occurs in the prologues spoken, in the manner of Gower's prologues in *Pericles*, by the Chorus Leaders before certain of the scenes, including the ballet *divertissement* of Dick Whittington and his cat. A fourth occurs in the verse assigned to the Plutocrat, and a fifth and sixth in the contrasting chants of Redshirts and Blackshirts in the same dialogue. Analogous to these chants but reminiscent of 'The Hollow Men' and the *Landscapes*, is another type occurring in the chants of the Workmen and of the Unemployed. Lastly there is the type occurring in the choruses proper (spoken unapocalyptically, though by seven men and ten women) personating 'the voice of the Church of God'; to it belong also the lines of the Rock himself. The effect of such variety, interspersed with a like variety of dumb shows with prose speeches, and with music, would be more pleasing if more systematic or, at least, coherent."[60]

But in *The Rock*, Eliot's demonstration of the new form is not very persuasive. The fluency and maturity comes with his next play *Murder in the Cathedral*, with the liberating effect of the unifying dramatic conception. But despite its weaknesses, *The Rock* is an important stage in the development of his dramatic career. It prepared Eliot for his coming masterpiece. D.E. Jones also, comparing the chorus in *The Rock* with those of *Murder in the Cathedral* says: "In the earlier play the style merely flutters; in the later it soars."[61]

NOTES AND REFERECES

Sweeney Agonistes

1. Williamson George. 1962. *A Reader's Guide to T.S. Eliot.* New York: The Noonday Press. 195.
2. Smith, Carol H. 1963. *T.S. Eliot's Dramatic Theory and Practice.* London: Oxford University Press. 57.
3. Jones, D.E. 1960. *The Plays of T.S. Eliot.* London: Routledge & Kegan Paul. 30.
4. Smith, Carol H. 1963. *T.S. Eliot's Dramatic Theory and Practice.* London: Oxford University Press. 58.
5. *Ibid.* 59.
6. *Ibid.* 58. Here he has quoted T.S. Eliot.
7. Jones, D.E. 1963. *The Plays of T.S. Eliot.* London: Routledge & Kegan Paul. 58-59.
8. Smith, Carol H. 1963. *T.S. Eliot's Dramatic Theory and Practice.* London: Oxford University Press. 58-59.
9. *Ibid.* 59.
10. Eliot, T.S. 1969. *The Complete Poems and Plays of T.S. Eliot.* London: Faber and Faber. 115.
11. Cornford, Francis M. *The Origin of Attic Comedy.* London, quoted in Smith, Carol H. 1963. *T.S. Eliot's Dramatic Theory and Practice.* London: Oxford University Press. 45.
12. Bennet, Arnold. *Journals.* Quoted in Sarkar, Subhas. *T.S. Eliot—The Dramatist.* New Delhi: Atlantic Publishers & Distributors (P) Ltd. 40.
13. Eliot, T.S. *The Complete Poems and Plays of T.S. Eliot.* London: Faber and Faber. 115.
14. *Ibid.*
15. *Ibid.*
16. Smith, Carol H. 1963. *T.S. Eliot's Dramatic Theory and Practice.* London: Oxford University Press. 64.
17. Eliot, T.S. 1969. *The Complete Poems and Plays of T.S. Eliot.* London: Faber and Faber. 116.
18. *Ibid.*
19. *Ibid.*
20. *Ibid.*
21. *Ibid.* 117.
22. *Ibid.*

23. *Ibid.*
24. *Ibid.*
25. *Ibid.*
26. *Ibid.*
27. *Ibid.*
28. *Ibid.*
29. *Ibid.* 118.
30. *Ibid.* 124.
31. Sarkar, Subhas. 2006. *T.S. Eliot—The Dramatist.* New Delhi: Atlantic Publishers & Distributors (P) Ltd. 40-41.
32. Eliot, T.S. *The Complete Poems and Plays of T.S. Eliot.* London: Faber and Faber. 121.
33. *Ibid.* 122.
34. *Ibid.* 123.
35. *Ibid.*
36. *Ibid.*
37. *Ibid.*
38. *Ibid.*
39. *Ibid.* 124.
40. Sarkar, Subhas. 2006. *T.S. Eliot—The Dramatist.* New Delhi: Atlantic Publishers & Distributors (P) Ltd. 35.
41. Smith, Carol H. 1963. *T.S. Eliot's Dramatic Theory and Practice.* London: Oxford University Press. 71.
42. Eliot, T.S. 1969. *The Complete Poems and Plays of T.S. Eliot.* London: Faber and Faber. 122.
43. *Ibid.*
44. *Ibid.*
45. Cornford, Francis M. *The Origin of Attic Comedy.* London. 188-89. Quoted in Smith, Carol H. 1963. *T.S. Eliot's Dramatic Theory and Practice.* London: Oxford University Press. 68.
46. Eliot, T.S. 1969. *The Complete Poems and Plays of T.S. Eliot.* London: Faber and Faber. 125.
47. Smith, Carol H. 1963. *T.S. Eliot's Dramatic Theory and Practice.* London: Oxford University Press. 72.
48. Eliot, T.S. 1969. *The Complete Poems and Plays of T.S. Eliot.* London: Faber and Faber. 126.
49. Jones, D.E. 1963. *The Plays of T.S. Eliot.* London: Routledge & Kegan Paul. 15. Quoted in Smith, Carol H. 1963. *T.S. Eliot's*

Dramatic Theory and Practice. London: Oxford University Press. 33.
50. Smith, Carol H. 1963. *T.S. Eliot's Dramatic Theory and Practice.* London: Oxford University Press. 55.
51. Eliot, T.S. 1963. *The Use of Poetry and the Use of Criticism.* 146-47. Quoted in Smith, Carol H. 1963. *T.S. Eliot's Dramatic Theory and Practice.* London: Oxford University Press. 54-55.
52. Bradbrook, M.C. 1965. *English Dramatic Form—A History of its Development.* London: Chatto & Windus. 165.
53. Smith, Carol H. 1963. *T.S. Eliot's Dramatic Theory and Practice.* London: Oxford University Press. 60.
54. *Ibid.* 61-62.
55. Sarkar, Subhas. 2006. *T.S. Eliot—The Dramatist.* New Delhi: Atlantic Publishers & Distributors (P) Ltd. 44.
56. Roy, V.K. 1979. *T.S. Eliot: Quest for Belief.* Delhi: Ajanta Publications. 219.
57. Singh, Parwati. 1988. *Character and Symbol in the Plays of T.S. Eliot.* Delhi: Capital Publishing House. 8.
58. Smith, Carol H. 1963. *T.S. Eliot's Dramatic Theory and Practice.* London: Oxford University Press. 72.
59. *Ibid.*
60. *Ibid.*
61. Jones, D.E. 1960. *The Plays of T.S. Eliot.* London: Routledge & Kegan Paul. 29-30.
62. Sharma, H.L. 1976. *T.S. Eliot, His Dramatic Theories.* New Delhi: S. Chand & Co. 110.
63. Eliot, T.S. 1964. *The Sacred Wood.* London: Metheun & Co. 70.
64. Eliot, T.S. 1969. *The Complete Poems and Plays of T.S. Eliot.* London: Faber and Faber. 122.
65. Seaars Jayne. *Mr Eliot's Agon (Philological Quarterly, XXXIV, 1955)* Quoted in Jones, D.E. 1960. *The Plays of T.S. Eliot.* London: Routledge & Kegan Paul. 28n.
66. Sharma, H.L. 1976. *T.S. Eliot, His Dramatic Theories.* New Delhi: S. Chand & Co. 48-49.
67. Melchiori, Giorgio. 1959. *The Tightrope Walkers.* London: Routledge & Kegan Paul. 121.
68. Raymond, Williams. 1954. *Drama from Ibson to Eliot.* London: Chatto & Windus. 225.
69. Melchiori, Giorgio. 1959. *The Tightrope Walkers.* London: Routledge & Kegan Paul. 121.

70. Bradbrook, M.C. 1965. *English Dramatic Form—A History of its Development*. London: Chatto & Windus. 162.

The Rock

1. Eliot, T.S. 1934. *The Prefatory Note to the Play, The Rock*. London: Faber and Faber. Quoted in Sarkar, Subhas. 2006. *T.S. Eliot—The Dramatist*. New Delhi: Atlantic Publishers & Distributions (P) Ltd. 41.
2. Brown, Martin. *From The Rock to the Confidential Clerk* in Neville Braybrook. 1958. *T.S. Eliot—A Symposium, for his Seventieth Birthday*. London: Rupert Hart-Davis. 57. Quoted in Sarkar, Subhas. 2006. *T.S. Eliot—The Dramatist*. New Delhi: Atlantic Publishers & Distributors (P) Ltd. 42.
3. Coghill, Nevill. Ed. 1963. *Murder in the Cathedral*. London: Oxford University Press. 15.
4. Singh, Parwati. 1988. *Character and Symbol in the Plays of T.S. Eliot*. New Delhi: Capital Publishing House. 14.
5. Jones, D.E. 1960. *The Plays of T.S. Eliot*. London: Routledge & Kegan Paul 39-45.
6. Eliot, T.S. 1969. *The Complete Poems and Plays of T.S. Eliot*. London: Faber and Faber. 147.
7. *Ibid.*
8. *Ibid.* 148.
9. *Ibid.* 149.
10. *Ibid.* 150.
11. Herbert, Michael. 2001. *York Notes on Selected Poems of T.S. Eliot*. First Indian Reprint London: York Press. 61-62.
12. Eliot, T.S. 1969. *The Complete Poems and Plays of T.S. Eliot*. London: Faber and Faber. 151.
13. *Ibid.* 152.
14. *Ibid.* 153.
15. Herbert, Michael. 2001. *York Notes on Selected Poems of T.S. Eliot*. First Indian Reprint. London: York Press. 63.
16. Eliot, T.S. 1969. *The Complete Poems and Plays of T.S. Eliot*. London: Faber and Faber. 154.
17. *Ibid.* 155.
18. *Ibid.* 156.
19. Herbert, Michael. 2001. *York Notes on Selected Poems of T.S. Eliot*. First Indian Reprint. London: York Press. 64-65.

20. Eliot, T.S. 1969. *The Complete Poems and Plays of T.S. Eliot.* London: Faber and Faber. 157.
21. *Ibid.*
22. *Ibid.* 158.
23. *Ibid.* 159.
24. *Ibid.*
25. Sarkar, Subhas. 2006. *T.S. Eliot—The Dramatist.* New Delhi: Atlantic Publishers & Distributers (P) Ltd. 44-45.
26. Jones, D.E. 1960. *The Plays of T.S. Eliot.* London: Routledge & Kegan Paul. 42.
27. Eliot, T.S. *The Rock.* Faber and Faber (1934), 43-44. Quoted in Jones, D.E. 1960. *The Plays of T.S. Eliot.* London: Routledge & Kegan Paul. 42-43.
28. Eliot, T.S. 1969. *The Complete Poems and Plays of T.S. Eliot.* London: Faber and Faber. 160.
29. *Ibid.*
30. *Ibid.* 161.
31. *Ibid.*
32. *Ibid.*
33. Herbert, Michael. 2001. *York Notes on Selected Poems of T.S. Eliot.* First Indian Reprint. London: York Press. 66.
34. Jones, D.E. 1960. *The Plays of T.S. Eliot.* London: Routledge & Kegan Paul. 44.
35. Eliot, T.S. 1969. *The Complete Poems and Plays of T.S. Eliot.* London: Faber and Faber. 163.
36. Jones, D.E. 1960. *The Plays of T.S. Eliot.* London: Routledge & Kegan Paul. 44.
37. Eliot, T.S. 1969. *The Complete Poems and Plays of T.S. Eliot.* London: Faber and Faber. 164.
38. Smith, Grover. 2000. *T.S. Eliot's Poetry and Plays.* Chicago: The University of Chicago Press. First Indian Reprint. Delhi: Doaba Publications. 178.
39. Eliot, T.S. 1969. *The Complete Poems and Plays of T.S. Eliot.* London: Faber and Faber. 165.
40. *Ibid.*
41. Jones, D.E. 1960. *The Plays of T.S. Eliot.* London: Routledge & Kegan Paul, 45.
42. Eliot, T.S. 1969. *The Complete Poems and Plays of T.S. Eliot.* London: Faber and Faber. 166.

43. Ibid.
44. Ibid. 167.
45. Herbert, Michael. 2001. *York Notes on Selected Poems of T.S. Eliot*, First Indian Reprint. London: York Press. 68.
46. Smith, Carol H. 1963. *T.S. Eliot's Dramatic Theory and Practice*. London: Oxford University Press. 84-85.
47. Ibid. 88.
48. Smith, Grover. *T.S. Eliot's Poetry and Plays*. Chicago: The University of Chicago Press. First Indian Reprint. Delhi: Doaba Publications. 177.
49. Smith, Carol H. 1963. *T.S. Eliot's Dramatic Theory and Practice*. London: Oxford University Press. 85-86.
50. Mathiessen, F.O. 1959. *The Achievement of T.S. Eliot*. New York: Oxford University Press. 161.
51. Ibid. 161-62.
52. Sarkar, Subhas. 2006. *T.S. Eliot—The Dramatist*. New Delhi: Atlantic Publishers & Distributors (P) Ltd. 45.
53. Eliot, T.S. 1959. *The Three Voices of Poetry in on Poetry and Poets*. London: Faber and Faber. 91.
54. Mathiessen, F.O. 1959. *The Achievement of T.S. Eliot*. New York: Oxford University Press. 162.
55. Jones, D.E. 1960. *The Plays of T.S. Eliot*. London: Routledge & Kegan Paul. 47.
56. Ibid. 46.
57. Smith, Carol H. 1963. *T.S. Eliot's Dramatic Theory and Practice*. London: Oxford University Press. 86.
58. Browne, E. Martin. *T.S. Eliot—A Symposium* ed. March and Tambimuttu. 197-98. Quoted in Jones, D.E. 1960. *The Plays of T.S. Eliot*. London: Routledge & Kegan Paul. 46-47.
59. Smith, Grover. *T.S. Eliot's Poetey and Plays*. Chicago: The University of Chicago Press. First Indian Reprint. Delhi: Doaba Publications. 174.
60. Ibid. 172-73.
61. Jones, D.E. 1960. *The Plays of T.S. Eliot*. London: Routledge & Kegan Paul. 47.

3 Murder in the Cathedral

Murder in the Cathedral, a poetic drama in two Acts, was written in 1935 for its opening performance at the Canterbury Festival in June 1935, in the Chapter House of Canterbury Cathedral, only a few yards from the site of the spot where Archbishop Thomas Becket was murdered in A.D. 1170. E. Martin Browne was the producer of the play and it is said that the title of the play was also suggested to Mr. Eliot by him. Like every other play of T.S. Eliot, the title of *Murder in the Cathedral* has a significant bearing on the theme of the drama. There is always an undertone of irony in the titles of Eliot's plays.

According to M.C. Bradbrook, "*Murder in the Cathedral* gratified Eliot's ten-year old ambition; it is also a landmark in English dramatic history; for it proved that English verse drama could still succeed, and Eliot's younger contemporaries hastened to follow him."[1] The play, in fact "forms a distinct milestone in the journey towards the resuscitation of a modern poetic drama. Here an author regarded by many of the younger generation as their chief master, turned to the theatre and sought to apply his characteristic style"[2] to the production of the play which became a class in itself. He exploited the tradition of mystery and morality plays which has been very strong in England and also the popularity of the life story of Thomas A. Becket whose name is familiar to almost every household in the country. He fused together the best of the Aeschylean tradition with the best from the Morality plays, pointing out at the same time the contemporary relevance of the situation.

The play has been set against the background of the 12th century England. It is a dramatization of an important historical event, that is, the murder of the Archbishop of Canterbury. A few months after the coronation of Henry II, his

Murder in the Cathedral

some time servant Thomas Becket was raised, through his influence, to the Chancellorship in 1155. The King and the Chancellor became inseparable friends.

After a few years occurred the death of the Primate Theobald, and thus the Seat of Canterbury fell vacant. The King decided to select Becket as the new Archbishop. No sooner did Thomas Becket become the Archbishop than the differences between the King and Archbishop got acuter on ecclesiastical matters. The dispute between Henry and Becket began with arguments respecting payment of the Sheriff's aid and the matter was debated at the Council of Woodstock in July 1163. There followed much more serious disagreement respecting jurisdiction over 'criminous clerks.' In the Council of Clarendon in January 1164, this issue broadened into a controversy. In the same year Thomas Becket went into exile and came back in December 1170, after an interval of seven years.

Becket's return and his welcome home after the years of exile were both very astonishing. At Canterbury the monks received him as an angel of God. Then, hot foot, he proceeded to renew his excommunication of the clergy who had taken part in the crowning of young Henry. These unfortunate priests and prelates travelled in a bunch to the King, who was in Normandy. They told a tale not only of an ecclesiastical challenge, but also of actual revolt and usurpation. They said that the Archbishop was ready to "tear the crown from the young King's head." At this, point the King got very angry and uttered before the nobles and knights. "What a pack of fools and cowards I have nourished in my house, that not one of them will avenge me of this turbulent Priest." At this insinuation four of the knights left the place and murdered the Archbishop (Becket) in Canterbury Cathedral. It is this historical episode that forms the subject matter of this play.

The play opens with the singing of the chorus of local Women of Canterbury. They have assembled in the Archbishop's Hall, adjoining the Canterbury Cathedral, drawn by some irresistible power to anticipate the coming events. An impulse of grave concern has dragged them there to witness 'some presage of an act' which remains as yet unknown to them:

"Some presage of an act
Which our eyes are compelled to witness, has forced our feet
Towards the Cathedral. We are forced to bear witness."[3]

The chorus laments the passing of the seasons from bountiful autumn to death like winter and has premonitions both of imminent treachery and of martyrdom. "The opening chorus of the play seems to set the tone of the ritual in the Greek fashion. In the ritual drama of the Greeks there is always the conception of the year as an anthropized being. The idea of agon or a contest as of life and death is illustrated in summer plenty and winter dearth. The life of the year—daemon, as it is reflected in Tragedy is often a story of Pride and Punishment. Each year commits the sin of Hubris (Pride) and is slain, consequently. But his act of slaying is also a sin, and hence comes the next year as Avenger. Thus the notion of inexorable fate is present in this conception."[4]

"Since Golden October declined into somber November
And the apples were gathered and stored and the land became
Brown sharp points of death in a waste of water and mud,
The New Year waits, breathes, waits whispers in darkness
While the labourer kicks off a muddy boot and stretches his hand to the fire
The New Year waits, destiny waits for the coming."[5]

"The dominant imagery of the primitive life; harvesting, seasonal cycle of death and rebirth, imagery of disgust and yearning for security, etc. makes the chorus sufficiently charged with poetic emotion and creates the proper setting for the drama of religious experience."[6] The women of Canterbury reflect that it is now seven years since the Archbishop fled from Canterbury. He had always been very kind to the common people. But they fear that things will not go well with him, should he return. They are apprehensive of some misery that might befall them:

Some malady is coming upon us. We wait, we wait,
And the saints and martyrs wait, for those who shall be martyrs and saints.[7]

Nonetheless, only God controls future event—and these they must await as passive witnesses as "Destiny waits in the hands of God, shaping the still unshapen."[8]

"For us, the poor, there is no action,
But only to wait and to witness."[9]

After the women retire, having sung the chorus three Priests attached to the Cathedral enter the scene and speak of the ceaseless intrigues and meetings abroad between the Pope and Henry II. The Priests condemn the temporal power for their 'greed and lust' and violence and duplicity. They also feel sorry for the poor who have lost their faith in God.

The conversation of the Priests is interrupted by the arrival of a Messenger who arrives with the news that the Archbishop has returned to England and is approaching the outskirts of Canterbury. The Messenger asks them to get ready to welcome him and inform that Thomas has been received with frenzied enthusiasm by people en route. The Priests anxiously ask the Messenger about Becket's relations with the King to which he replies that the two proud men have not had a genuine reconciliation—some sort of truce has been patched up between them, which may not last long.

All the Priests, however, wonder whether the arrival of the Archbishop would mean war or peace. But the chorus of Canterbury Women is certain of the impending doom, and wish that Becket again returns to France because according to them death is waiting for him in Canterbury.

"O Thomas, return, Archbishop; return, return to France.
Return. Quickly. Quietly. Leave us to perish in quiet.
You come with applause, you come with rejoicing,
but you come bringing death into Canterbury;
A doom on the house, a doom on yourself, a doom on the world."[10]

But the Priests rebuke the women for their foolish babbling and urge them to forget their fears and join in 'a hearty welcome to our good Archbishop.'

Just while the discussion was going on, Thomas Becket—the Archbishop—enters and requests them to have peace. He declares that there may be much wisdom in what they were saying. God regulates our actions and we must submit to his will. He adds that they know and don't know that action is suffering and suffering is action:

"...Neither does the agent suffer,
Nor the patient act. But both are fixed
In an eternal action, an eternal patience.
To which all must consent that it may be willed
And which all must suffer that they may will it.
That the pattern may subsist, for the pattern is the action
And the suffering, that the wheel may turn and still
Be forever still."[11]

These words of Becket reflect the idea that, "Humanity is tied to a vast pattern, like the Buddhist wheel; in part passive, in part active, in its turning. It is submission in suffering, submission in willing suffering which is part of the eternal design."[12]

The Priests, then apologize to Thomas for their meager welcome, but say that the Archbishop's seven years of exile has been a period of emptiness for them all and they have had plenty of opportunity to prepare their hearts for this great day. But he may be pleased to find his rooms in the same nice condition in which he had left them. But there is great irony of fate in Becket's reply when he says, "And will try to leave them in order as I find them."[13]

Although grateful for their kind attention, Becket expects to have little rest or leisure in Canterbury. On his return trip he had been surrounded by spies and rebellious bishops who would have killed him had the Dean of Salisbury not saved him. Nonetheless they will continue to hover like hawks, waiting for an opportune moment to attack.

Then the Archbishop has his encounter with the Tempters. The play is lifted to a higher plane of action when four Tempters, who represent the innermost working of Becket's mind, are introduced. The First Tempter reminds him of his old carnal pleasure he had once enjoyed as a friend of the King. So now when he has reconciled with the King he should again allow clergy and laity to relax 'in mirth and sportfulness.'[14] But Thomas ignores him and dismisses him telling "you come twenty years too late."[15]

Then the Second Tempter comes to tempt Thomas of secular power. He tells him that it was his mistake to resign the Chancellor and accept the Archbishopric. He advises Thomas to give up the pretence of priestly power for the power and glory of the Crown. It was no good to be a self-bound servant of the powerless Pope or like an old stag circled with hounds. But the Archbishop refuses to forget and forego his celestial duty for the political power.

Then the Third Tempter enters and confesses that he is no courtier or intriguer but a plain speaking "country-keeping lord who minds his own business."[16] He urges him to throw his lot with the barons against the Crown, because such a coalition would strengthen the hands of the Church. But again Thomas declines to accept the suggestions of the Tempter.

Then enters the Fourth Tempter, who admires Thomas's unbending will and urges him to do his duty and not to look to temporal power which is ephemeral, while Thomas holds in his hand the reins of everlasting spiritual glory, by seeking the way to martyrdom.

"Think of glory after death
When king is dead there's another king
And one more king is another reign
King is forgotten, when another shall come
Saint and martyr rule from the tomb."[17]

As a Saint in heaven, Becket will be able to look down at his persecutors suffering timeless torments in hell. Thomas recoils from this suggestions also, but the Tempter points out that he is simply repeating what the Archbishop himself has often dreamt of and echoes Becket's own thesis that action and suffering are synonymous.

Commenting on Becket's response to the Tempters Hugh Kenner says, "...Becket readily puts aside three Tempters, whose function resembles that of the visions left behind on the Ash-Wednesday stairs; indeed one of them recalls to the 'Old Tom, gay Tom'[18].... But the Fourth Tempter, whom he does not expect, shakes his composure."[19]

Thereafter, the Chorus comments on the oppressive atmosphere and the Four Tempters declare that the life of man is nothing but a series of disappointments. Becket, they say has deceived himself with delusions of his own grandeur, a victim of his own pride and has thus become an enemy of the society as well as his own enemy. The Chorus, the Priests and the Tempters, alternately refer to the impossibility of warding off death by taking advance precautions: "Death has a hundred hands and walks by a thousand ways."[20] The Women of Canterbury again address the Archbishop directly warning him of the impending calamity:

"O Thomas Archbishop, save us, save yourself
That we may be saved.
Destroy yourself and we are destroyed."[21]

Thomas now realizes that his future course of action is clear. He reflects how the Fourth Tempter, in urging him to "do the right deed for the wrong reason"[22] had suggested the greatest treason of all. Addressing the audience Becket stresses that the Tempters are now finally defeated and that his course is to submit himself entirely to the will of God and to await with a humble heart whatever decision God may choose to make.

"Now is my way clear, now is the meaning plain:
Temptation shall not come in this kind again.
The last temptation is the greatest treason:
To do the right deed for the wrong reason."[23]

There is no escaping from one's sins by consciously seeking the way to martyrdom, and subsequently in the Christmas Sermon we learn in some detail how martyrdom is never the design of men.

During the interval preceding this announcement the Chorus of the Women has demonstrated how life can be regarded as something more than a cheat and a disappointment, though without excessive optimism. They do not pass from "unreality to unreality."[24]

"We are not ignorant women,
We know what we must expect and not expect
We know of oppression and torture,
We know of extortion and violence,
Destitution, disease,
The old without fire in winter,
The child without milk in summer."[25]

"This catalogue of misfortunes does not suggest to them a facile disillusionment:"[26]

"And meanwhile we have gone on living
Living and Partly living,
Picking together the pieces,
Gathering faggots at nightfall,
Building a partial shelter
For sleeping, and eating and drinking and laughter."[27]

"The conflict is between the values of the world and of the spirit; as seen by the Chorus of the Women of Canterbury, the Four Tempters, the Four Knights and focused in Becket's own choice. And his leading temptation is one the Christian forms of *hubris*, pride in one's own humility."[28] "A sense of duality—of the simultaneity of existence on the material and spiritual plane, is a significant aspect of Eliot's *Theory of Poetic Drama*; and this double pattern of life is woven *Murder in the Cathedral* by the Chorus."[29]

Thus Part I of the play closes. The sermon delivered by Thomas on the Christmas morning of 1170 forms an interlude between the two parts of the play. In the sermon he analyses what exactly the wrong reason for martyrdom is. According to him, "A Christian martyrdom is never an accident, for saints are not made by accident. Still less is a Christian martyrdom, the effect of a man's will to become a Saint, as a man by willing and contriving may become a ruler of men. A martyrdom is always the design of God, for his love of men, to warn them and to lead them, to bring them back to His ways. It is never the design of man; for the true martyr is he who has become the instrument of God, who has lost his own will in the will of God and who no longer desires anything for himself, not even the glory of being a martyr."[30]

Becket's Christmas sermon provides the audience an opportunity for direct participation in the act of worship and spiritual communion. "Thomas's sermon...is spoken directly to the audience—for this of course, Eliot had precedent in his medieval model, since *Everyman* concludes with a sermon on pride."[31]

The second part of the play also begins with the chorus sung by the Women of Canterbury, who are sensing a premonition: "Between Christmas and Easter what shall be done?"[32] This time the Chorus gives a clear indication of the murder of the Archbishop.

"The starved crow sits in the field, attentive;
and in the wood
The owl rehearses the hollow note of death."[33]

Then the three Priests enter in a procession and in turn announce the passing of the days, carrying banners of St. Stephen, the first Christian martyr and St. John the apostle and the holy innocent respectively.

Then the four Knights come. They come with terrific speed. They ask for the Archbishop and pretend to have brought a very urgent message from the King. When the Archbishop appears before them, they abuse him and accuse him of revolting against the King. Thomas refutes this, but the Knights continue their rash accusations and ask him to reinstate and absolve the Bishops who have been suspended by the Pope. They present the King's command for this. But Thomas refuses to accept the orders, which infuriates the Knight. They threaten him with life but Thomas holds fast in the name of Church and says:

"I submit my cause to the judgment of Rome.
But if you kill me, I shall rise from my tomb
To submit my cause before God's throne."[34]

At this the Knights become furious and ask Priests to restrain their master from disobedience and leave. As the Knights exit the Women of Canterbury reappear. This time they smell death in Canterbury. In their opinion everything is predestined. Thomas also warns the Women about there being something painful in the womb of futurity. The situation is tense. The Priests also warn him about the return of the Knights, but Thomas is formidable. He places duty above danger.

"All my life they have been coming, these feet all my life
I have waited. Death will come only when I am worthy
And if I am worthy, there is no danger
I have therefore only to make perfect my will."[35]

But the Priests feel highly nervous and advise Thomas to flee to the Altar. But Thomas refuses to take flight since death will only come to him when God considers him worthy of it.

As the moment of martyrdom approaches the Chorus has a vision of horror beyond all horrors that life can bring. Meanwhile, inside the cathedral, the Priests have barred the doors since the Knights are like ferocious beasts. But Becket is not prepared to turn the sanctuary into a fortress and gets the doors opened. Now the four Knights, who are the sordid instrument of the eternal design, burst into the scene and the murder is completed and Becket dies with the name of God and the blessed Saints on his lips.

So, Becket exemplifies the true meaning of humility, sacrifice and suffering in his life and martyrdom. He embraced the dictum 'action is suffering and suffering is action' in the truest sense. Grover Smith writes about the theme of the play: "To suffer or endure is to live; to live is inevitably to act. All who act rightly, moreover, are martyrs, witnesses; for right action requires humility, the refinement of will under oppression."[36]

Again the Chorus that calls Death as 'God's silent servant' calls their Archbishop's murder as beastly and inhuman. "Coming hard upon the agony of the martyr and the tremendous outburst of the chorus in which tears 'drown the wind'...the Knights seek skilfully, using the techniques of modern political oratory, to tempt the audience into admitting the reasonableness of their action and to acknowledge that they (the audience) are involved in it, since they have benefited from it.... But the impact of Thomas's sacrifice remains: the Priests return and help to recover the mood of the martyrdom in a chastened form. From a threnody for the Archbishop in minor key, the recovered verse-form modulates to the major hymn of praise and thanksgiving for the new saint of Canterbury with which the play ends."³⁷

In fact, the chorus keeps us in direct contact with the celebration of the act of martyrdom, and finally the choir sings the glory of God and prays to him, which ends with the following note:

"Lord have mercy upon us.
Christ have mercy upon us.
Lord have mercy upon us.
Blessed Thomas, pray for us."³⁸

Carol H. Smith aptly remarks, "In *Murder in the Cathedral*, he (Eliot) had been successful in sustaining two distinct levels of meaning, the surface actions leading to the martyrdom of Becket and beneath the surface analogies with the suffering and glory of Christ."³⁹

Analyzing the various motifs underlying the play Hugh Kenner says, "There are in fact three motifs in *Murder in the Cathedral*, not intertwined but competing for prominence: the change in the orientation of Becket's will, which makes the play so useful a commentary on *Ash Wednesday*; the strife, still active in Eliot's poetic imagination because not wholly realized in *The Rock*, between secularism and the will of God; and the motif which the mere conditions of acted drama could not but thrust into prominence, the death of a valiant man. It is a remarkable first play, containing enough chaos to animate three more plays. It animated instead, in the same year, a remarkable meditative poem that stirred into life among the play's unrealized motifs and rejected scraps: *Burnt Noton*."⁴⁰

However, the central theme of the play is not just the dramatization of the death of Becket. "In fact Eliot's conception of Becket is not so much inspired by history as by his interest in Christian theology. His purpose has been to drive home the meaning of martyrdom and its application to life."⁴¹ It is a deep searching study of the significance of martyrdom, in its strict ancient sense. Eliot concentrates here on death and martyrdom, sin and evil. "The significance of sainthood and martyrdom— is presented in terms of different levels of symbols used in the speeches of different groups of characters and provides a key to the understanding of its multiple layers of significance. This involves, first, a study of the choric utterances as defining the attitude of the common people to the killing of Becket. Next come the speeches of the protagonist himself which indicate that the motivation of his action is seeking martyrdom. Whereas the speeches of the priests signify the point of view of the Church, those of the tempters represent voices and echoes of Becket, arising from some *Terrain Inconnu* of Becket's psyche. The knights express the feudal attitude towards the fight between the church and the state."[42]

"Eliot refers to the chorus of Women of Canterbury in the list of characters. They may be said to constitute the formal chorus yet all the other characters, except the protagonist, stand in groups. There are three priests of the Cathedral, four Tempters and four Knights and they have all a choric function to fulfil, for each of them represents the point of view of a group."[43] Though the Charwomen of Canterbury constitute the formal chorus, such characters as priests and knights stand in groups and are also more or less choral figures. Eliot hardly makes any attempt to differentiate them as characters and individuals. The only difference is that of moods, views and functions. In this respect Eliot's play shows a close resemblance with the Moralities. Herein only the hero, Thomas Becket, is an historical character; the rest of the cast is made up of abstractions.

D.E. Jones also says, "The elements of spiritual conflict in Thomas are objectified in a massive antiphony of three choral groups."[44] The priests represent the reaction of churchmen who are not saints to the realisation that there is a saint in their midst. The speeches of the priests are not as rich in imagery as those of Women of Canterbury. Perhaps because they are attached to an institution their reactions tend to be more formal than those of common fold. The Knights are also not individuals; they represent 'brute force.' They become symbols of no specified authority, but rather of general tyranny of the material over the spiritual, of the temporal over the eternal. This impression is further enhanced by the stylized, by almost choric nature of their speeches. How they speak, makes it entirely appropriate to play the murder itself in the non-realistic manner of traditional pantomime and this in itself suggests a ritual murder. The martyrdom is suddenly illuminated as a symbol of the death of Christ, as Thomas's.

"Thus all the characters of Eliot can be divided into three groups—those in whom the tougher self is already well developed, so that they not only have a firm grasp of the true values, but can also initiate the worthy into vision; those in whom this better-self has a high potential which is developed during the course of the play; and those in whom it can never develop and come into its own. The three groups may be characterised as *Helpers, Seekers* and *Blind* respectively. The first has already attained *Paradise*; the second are in *Purgatory*; the third must remain in *Hell*."[45] Thomas Becket in *Murder in the Cathedral* combines the role of the helper and the seeker, but for entirely different reasons.

Like a Greek tragedy, "the play opens significantly with a speech by a Chorus of the Women of Canterbury and like its Attic counterpart this chorus gives us a good deal of information about time, place and potentiality of the scenes."[46] It may assume a prominent role in the action or may serve merely as an observer or a commentator. Eliot's chorus performs a function somewhere between these two. The Women of Canterbury are primarily observers and commentators but their reaction to what they observe assumes significance. This is often conveyed in simple atmospheric term:

"Are we drawn by danger? Is it the knowledge of safety that draws our feet
Towards the Cathedral?"[47]

We are at once made aware that there is both danger and safety for the Charwomen in moving towards the Cathedral. Though hyper-conscious of it, the Chorus knows that the danger only indirectly threatens them:

The women introduce themselves as "the poor, the poor women of Canterbury,"[48] and later refer to themselves at their daily task as "the scrubbers and sweepers of Canterbury."[49] They are "the small folk drawn into the pattern of fate, the small folk who live among small things,"[50] "living and partly living."[51] When we first see them, they have a premonition of what is to come and of their part in it, and they fear that they will not prove equal to the task. They fear even more, the impending "disturbance of the quiet seasons"[52] the irruption of the unknown, the uncontrollable, into the familiar round of their lives, which they have carefully ordered to create a feeling of security, conveniently forgetting what should make them question this false sense of safety and permanence. They would prefer "to pass unobserved,"[53] "succeeding in avoiding notice."[54] So, even though they recognize that what is about to happen is the design of God, they think of it as an illness, something they would rather do without.

To witness in the Christian sense means, however, not just to see but to be involved, to make a public avowal of faith in action as well as in words, and in their fear at the possible consequences of action, they appeal rhetorically to Thomas and implore him to return to France.[55] As the Tempters gather their forces for a united attack on Thomas, the chorus's fear mounts, through an oppressive sense of the evil at war with the good, in him, "The earth is heaving to parturition of issue of hell,"[56] to a sudden panic at the possibility that the "Lords of Hell"[57] will triumph. They thus acknowledge that their spiritual welfare depends upon Thomas.[58]

In the chorus, which opens Part II, they admit the need for his sacrifice, but of their own part in the design—the consent implicit in standing by and doing nothing to prevent the murder. They are keenly ashamed: "Nothing is possible but the shamed swoon of those consenting to the last humiliation."[59] They seem to have consented to "what is woven on the loom of fate"[60] and have now reconciled to the "eternal patience" and acknowledged their responsibility for the imminent death of Thomas by recognizing that they will be involved in the sin of the murderers. They see "the white face of Death, God's silent servant."[61] Even "this instant eternity of evil"[62] and the evil of their timid inaction will be turned into something good for themselves and all men through the martyrdom which God has ordained.

As the moment of martyrdom approaches, however, the chorus has a vision of horror of the void, "more horrid than active shapes of hell"[63] and they picture the fate they can expect unless atonement is made. From it the women turn to the comfort of Christ's sacrifice about to be renewed in the martyrdom of Thomas. By the end of the play they have arrived at a full understanding of the significance of Thomas's death. They experience the moment of "painful joy" prophesied by Thomas and acknowledge that his sacrifice was made on their behalf and finally thank God, "Who hast given such blessings to Canterbury."[64] Thus under the impact of the martyrdom, they have moved from apathy and evasion to a lively faith and humble acceptance.

Thus, the Chorus of the Women of Canterbury almost echoes the feelings of the audience. As Cleanth Brooks has rightly remarked "Into the cries of the chorus he (Eliot) has poured the tragic experience of suffering humanity, caught in the grip of a secret cause: "We are forced to bear witness,"[65] while according to Helen Gardner "The chorus becomes humanity confronted by the mystery of inequity and the mystery of holiness."[66] The chorus, also, provides both background and counterpoint to the action, and it is through its reaction to the events of the martyrdom of Thomas, through its opposition and final reconciliation, that the tension and very powerful atmosphere are built up and maintained. Thus the chorus stands for the "religious conscience of humanity."[67]

According to John Peter, "the position of the chorus is ambivalent. At one stage they are simply the poor women of Canterbury, at another level the Chorus are transparently more than their natural selves. Like their equivalents in Greek tragedy, they present a commentary on the action, anticipating and preparing us for developments, rousing us with their passionate dithyrambs, to participate wholeheartedly in the emotional cries that arise, supplying the action with a background that is like music, all pervasive. It is in this second role that they now speak of moments of vision 'in a shaft of sunlight' and in as a flash of clairvoyance that their concluding catastrophe to December is made."[68]

"Shall the Son of Man be born again in the litter of scorn?"[69]

But Eliot has not just copied Aeschylus; he has given the chorus a new significance in the light of the Christian dispensation. In a talk, broadcast in the year after the first production of *Murder in the Cathedral*, Eliot remarked, "in making use of (the chorus) we do not aim to copy Greek drama. There is a good deal about the Greek theatre that we do not know and never shall know. But we know that some of its conventions cannot be ours. The characters frequently talk too long; the chorus has too much to say and holds up the action; usually not enough happens; and the Greek notion of climax is not ours. But the chorus has always fundamentally the same uses. It mediates between the action and the audience; it intensifies the action by projecting its emotional consequences so that we as the audience see it doubly, by seeing its effect on other people."[70]

"To this end, Eliot restored the full-throated chorus of Greek tragedy after centuries in which it was reduced to a single expositor of action. He has, in fact, gone back to the fountainhead of European drama and restored the Aeschylean form. He has used the chorus to open out the action into its full significance, as nobody else has done since Aeschylus."[71]

In Aeschylus the chorus has a character of its own. It consists of elders of Argos, or Libation bearers, or some such personages but for the most part it is just the author's mouthpiece, his principal means of conveying his vision of the significance of action. In *Murder in the Cathedral,* the chorus is much farther individualised. This is due less perhaps to the influence of naturalism and the modern emphasis on individuality than to the implications of Christianity, with its simultaneous emphasis on the precious uniqueness of the individual and the importance of the spiritual community. The chorus represents, in effect, the great mass of individuals, which Christ came to save. "We acknowledge ourselves as type of the common man...." The martyrdom of Becket is likewise on their behalf. The choruses embody their experience, rather than the author's view of the action. Of course they speak with his fullness of utterance, not with the limited idiom of real "scrubbers and sweepers." But this discrepancy is not far removed from the normal convention of dramatic poetry; what difference there is, can be largely accounted for, in terms of the convention of the communal speech. They are giving expression to communal feeling, which usually runs deeper than individual feeling, though it is not usually articulate. The articulateness is poetic illumination, differing from the normal convention of dramatic poetry only in degree.[72]

Eliot uses the chorus in *Murder in the Cathedral*, in part, according to Greek practice as an expository devices:

"Seven years and the summer is over
Seven years since the Archbishop left us,
He who was always kind to his people."[73]

But at times he goes even beyond this to enhance the potential of the chorus. As Williams Raymond observes "the function is merged in larger method, for which the tradition lives; the chorus becomes a link between ritual and believers; chorus is choir; the articulate voice of the body of worshippers":

Forgive us, O lord, we acknowledge ourselves as type
of the common man,
Of the men and women who shut the door and sit by the fire.[74]

The dramatic possibilities of this function of the chorus may have been suggested to Eliot by the Greek drama, but the dramatic realisation is in terms of the Christian ritual, the accepted, familiar relationships of priests, choir and congregation. Thus, a convention of choral speech, which is of great dramatic value, not only is, not an unfamiliar barrier, but also is the actual convention of participation. The convention is more; it is the actual form of the play. It embodies one of the principal dramatic movements, from the early,

"For us thought there is no action,
but only to wait and to witness"[75]

through the median:
"In our veins our bowels our skulls as well"[76]
to the final—
"...the blood of the martyrs and the agony of the saints
Is upon our heads"[77]
"a movement from passivity of surrender to participation."[78]

As Peacock Reynold also points out, "In *Murder in the Cathedral*, ritual belongs both to the inner structure of the play and to its performance. Through creating direct links at various points with his audience the poet has made his work into a continuous invitation to celebrate in religious fellowship the spiritual triumph of saint.... The drama becomes again an instrument of community."[79]

Thus not only is the full-throated chorus of Greek tragedy restored, as we have, seen its original function is enlarged in the light of the Christian liturgy. It represents the common people and mediates between them and the action, as the Greek drama, but also 'chorus is Choir' as Raymond Williams notes 'the articulate voice of the body of worshippers.' Now this element of ritual in the form of liturgy which runs as the underpattern of all his play, draws the audience almost unconsciously to a group participation and responsibility.

"The fusion of these elements of Christian drama of the Middle Ages with the pre-Christian drama of the Greeks yields a highly original form. Although nearer to Aeschylean tragedy than to any intervening form, it has been perfectly adapted to Christian theology and is very much of its time.... Yet it has also a functional simplicity which is particularly twentieth century...."[80] "A queer amalgam of Greek and Christian ideas as manifest in the ritual of Becket's martyrdom—his acceptance of death and almost the attic representation of the Choric utterances and the broad outline of the plot, offer a structure of emotions which appeal both to the religious people as well as to the secular audience of the commercial theatre."[81]

"In fact, Eliot has worked out a scheme of Objective Correlative for his dramas by fashioning his plots under the shadow of Greek myths, and providing an underpattern of liturgy for all of them.... One can easily find a parallel between the story of Becket in his cathedral and that of Oedipus in the sacred wood. The hero of Eliot's *Murder in the Cathedral* as well as the hero of Sophocles *Oedipus at Colonus* maintain the same attitude in the beginning. In their opening speech both the heroes maintain the attitude that patience is the lesson of suffering."[82]

As Prof. Murray observes, "In *Murder in the Cathedral*, T.S. Eliot has returned to the most primitive form of tragedy on the model of the earlier plays of Aeschylus in which there is one great situation, the poet steeping our mind with almost one or two sudden flashes of action passing over it."[83] Choruses in *Murder in the Cathedral* are aptly used and are in line with old Greek conception of tragedy. They are of great significance. They make us forget the imperfections of versification in the dialogue. In fact the use of choruses strengthened the dramatic power and concealed the defects of Eliot's theatrical technique.[84]

"The real drama of the play" says Helen Gardner, "is to be found in fact, where the greatest poetry lies—in the Choruses. The change, which is the life of drama, is there from the terror of the supernatural expressed, in the opening, to the rapturous recognition of the glory displayed in the creation of the earth, in the last."[85]

The most noteworthy role of the chorus in the play is that they develop the action of the play. Without them the plot of the play would have suffered a lot of suffocation and strangulation. Both the beginning and the end of the action in the play are conducted by the chorus. They initiate, conclude, comment on, and analyse the action of the play. They develop the plot, keep its continuity and knit various actions into one composite fibre. At times they perform the function of chronicler, of a critic and of a reformer. The choruses also act as indicators or foretellers of future action. They acquaint the audience with the coming events and retrospect the past events. The Chorus of Canterbury Women are also marked for the tragic and philosophic comments they make in the play. The speeches of the chorus are sometimes both profound and vigorous, combining the vigour of thought with the vigour of expression.

According to F.O. Mathiessen, "One of the most conspicuous technical triumphs in all Eliot's poetry is in the choruses that were designed to be spoken by the working women of Canterbury. Here he carried further his experiments in finding verse forms suitable to ritualistic drama. He had no living stage tradition upon which to draw, but he believed that a chorus could still perform something of the same fundamental function that it had for Greeks. It could mediate between the action and the audience; it could intensify the action by projecting its emotional consequences so that we as audience see it doubly by seeing its effect on other people."[86]

However, it is with chorus that Eliot is poetically most successful. The poetry uttered by the chorus hides most of Eliot's theatrical weakness and such other weaknesses as of plot and characterisation. Accounting for the use of the chorus, T.S. Eliot himself gives the following reasons for depending so heavily on the chorus in the play: "There were two reasons for this, which in the circumstances justified it. The first was that the essential action of the play—both the historical facts and the matter, which I invented—were limited. A man come home foreseeing that the will be killed, and he is killed. I did not want to increase the number of characters, I did not want to write a chronicle of 12th century politics, nor did I want to tamper unscrupulously with the meagre records as Tennyson did (in introducing fair Rosamund, and in suggesting that Becket had been crossed in love in early youth). I wanted to concentrate on death end martyrdom. The introduction of a chorus of excited and sometimes hysterical women reflecting in their emotion the significance of the action, helped wonderfully. The second reason was this: that a poet writing for the first time for the stage, is much more at home in choral verse than in dramatic dialogue. This, I felt sure, was something I could do, and perhaps the dramatic weaknesses would be somewhat covered up by the cries of women. The use of a chorus strengthened the power, and concealed the defects of my theatrical technique. For this reason I decided that next time I would try to integrate the chorus more closely into the play."[87]

As to the relevance of music in the language of the drama, Eliot states that it 'intensifies our experiment.' According to him there are things that can be expressed in music, which will be difficult, otherwise, to express in ordinary speech. Eliot does not, however, love music for its own sake. It is not an end in itself. It becomes an instrument of bringing home to the auditors 'a comprehensiveness' which is beyond the mere word. Besides this, the presence of rhythm—the primal force in music sends people back to an elemental basis, the pulse, the heartbeat, so essential for itself. Music in this sense expands our elemental impulses; widens our emotional selves; and leaves us better and stronger human beings. It also helps us impose what Eliot calls 'a credible order upon ordinary reality.'

Again, it is with the chorus that Eliot is poetically most successful. "The choruses owe much to the rhythm of Biblical verse, with its simplicity of syntax, emphatic repetitions and rhythmical variety. It is important to observe in this connection, the difference between the meters of dialogue and choral meters. Choric speaking must be emphatic or the sense is lost: it must keep time, and cannot indulge in too much variation of speed and tone. Many voices speaking together are incapable of the subtle modulations of a single voice, and of the innumerable variations from a regular material base that make up the music of poetry. On the other hand, if the meter is too regular, choral speaking will soon reduce it to the monotony of sing-song. Choric verse must, therefore, itself be written in free meters; the necessary variety must be inherent in the metrical structure, in variation, in the length of line, and the length of the breath unit. In short, where verse-dialogue approximates to speech, choric verse must approximate to chant."[88] And Eliot must skilfully observe in his verse these differences. He makes his chorus chant different verse from that which the hero speaks; and he makes his hero utter the verse which the Knights or the Priests or even the Tempters do not utter.

"Eliot has kept the versification of Everyman as a model before him to distinguish his verse from that of the Nineteenth century and has skilfully avoided the use of too much iambic. But his clever use of alliteration and occasional rhyme has decidedly a positive influence in heightening the tone of the drama.... In fact the strength of Eliot's play lies to a great extent in versification. Through careful selection of words, modulation of stress and variation of rhymes Eliot has been able to create the necessary moods and situations of the drama."[89] Grover Smith also says that, "Much of the poetry spoken by the chorus has a comparatively quick rhythm, despite the inevitable blurring of syllables which group recitation would cause; in actual staging, however, the lines are allotted to antiphonal voices."[90]

According to T.R. Henn, "The verse has the obsessive swelling effect of a Vedic chant, in which the words, opposing each other in the paradoxes proper to ritual of a certain kind, and hence perhaps too vast for the tragic scale, overwhelm us with a kind of grey cloud:

> They know and do not know, what it is to act or suffer.
> They know and do not know, that acting is suffering
> And suffering is action. Neither does the actor suffer
> Nor the patient act. Both are fixed
> In an eternal action, an eternal patience
> To which all must consent that it may be willed
> And which all must suffer that they may will it
> That the pattern may subsist, for the pattern is the action
> And the suffering, that the wheel may turn and still
> Be forever still.[91]

We could deduce, even if we did not know it from other sources, Mr. Eliot's intense interest in the Upanishads. The subtlety and close texture of the verse (the subtle play on *patient-patience, still-still*) are self-evident: but it is worthwhile to pause for a moment to consider what Eliot is saying through his mouthpiece Becket."[92]

"Historically, dramatically, structurally and poetically, the Chorus has a great significance in *Murder in the Cathedral*. It unfolds the action; it develops it. It comments on it and philosophises its contents. More than this it enhances the verse of the play. Its cries are the best pieces of dramatic poetry ever written in English. It strengthens the dramatic skill of the author and conceals the defects of his theatrical technique. In fact, it is an integral part of the play."[93] As David E. Jones says, "The Choruses were the fruit of the previous experimentation in *The Rock*. They are perhaps the greatest things in a great play. There is nothing else like them in English, to my knowledge."[94]

Thus the Chorus in the *Murder in the Cathedral* shows a positive advances by Eliot, in his dramatic techniques, where according to E. Martin Browne the Chorus becomes 'a full partner in the drama' and besides retaining its conventional role, assumes a new dimension.

NOTES AND REFERENCES

1. Bradbrook, M.C. 1965. *English Dramatic Form—A History of its Development*. London: Chatto & Windus. 163.
2. Nicoll, Allardyce. 1958. *British Drama*. London: George G. Harrap and Co. Ltd. 481.
3. Eliot, T.S. 1969. *The Complete Poems and Plays of T.S. Eliot*. London: Faber and Faber. 239.
4. Sarkar, Subhas. 2006. *T.S. Eliot—The Dramatist*. New Delhi: Atlantic Publishers & Distributors (P) Ltd. 100.
5. Eliot, T.S. 1969. *The Complete Poems and Plays of T.S. Eliot*. London: Faber and Faber. 239.
6. Sarkar, Subhas. 2006. *T.S. Eliot—The Dramatist*. New Delhi: Atlantic Publishers & Distributors (P) Ltd. 108.
7. Eliot, T.S. 1969. *The Complete Poems and Plays of T.S. Eliot*. London: Faber and Faber. 240.
8. *Ibid*.
9. *Ibid*.
10. *Ibid*.
11. *Ibid*. 245.
12. Henn, T.R. 1956. *The Harvest of Tragedy*. London: Methuen & Co. Ltd. 222.
13. Eliot, T.S. 1969. *The Complete Poems and Plays of T.S. Eliot*. London: Faber and Faber. 245.
14. *Ibid*. 247.
15. *Ibid*.
16. *Ibid*. 250.
17. *Ibid*. 254.
18. *Ibid*. 246.

19. Kenner, Hugh. 1965. *The Invisible Poet: T.S. Eliot*. University Paperbacks. London: Metheun & Co. Ltd. 236-37.
20. Eliot, T.S. 1969. *The Complete Poems and Plays of T.S. Eliot*. London: Faber and Faber. 256.
21. *Ibid*. 258.
22. *Ibid*.
23. *Ibid*.
24. Kenner, Hugh. 1965. *The Invisible Poet: T.S. Eliot*. University Paperbacks. London: Metheun & Co. Ltd. 240.
25. Eliot, T.S. 1969. *The Complete Poems and Plays of T.S. Eliot*. London: Faber and Faber. 257.
26. Kenner, Hugh. 1965. *The Invisible Poet: T.S. Eliot*. University Paperbacks. London: Metheun & Co. Ltd. 240.
27. Eliot, T.S. 1969. *The Complete Poems and Plays of T.S. Eliot*. London: Faber and Faber. 257.
28. Henn, T.R. 1956. *The Harvest of Tragedy*. London: Methuen & Co. Ltd. 221.
29. Sarkar, Subhas. 2006. *T.S. Eliot—The Dramatist*. New Delhi: Atlantic Publishers & Distributors (P) Ltd. 107.
30. Eliot, T.S. 1969. *The Complete Poems and Plays of T.S. Eliot*. London: Faber and Faber. 261.
31. Bradbrook, M.C. 1965. *English Dramatic Form—A History of its Development*. London: Chatto & Windus. 170.
32. Eliot, T.S. 1969. *The Complete Poems and Plays of T.S. Eliot*. London: Faber and Faber. 263.
33. *Ibid*.
34. *Ibid*. 269.
35. *Ibid*. 271.
36. Smith, Grover. 2000. *T.S. Eliot's Poetry and Plays*. Chicago: The University of Chicago Press. First Indian Reprint. Delhi: Doaba Publications. 196.
37. Methuen's Study-Aid. 1971. *Notes on T.S. Eliot's Murder in the Cathedral*. London: Metheun & Co. Ltd. 31.
38. Eliot, T.S. 1969. *The Complete Poems and Plays of T.S. Eliot*. London: Faber and Faber. 282.
39. Smith, Carol H. *T.S. Eliot's Dramatic Theory and Practice*. Quoted in Sarkar, Sunil Kumar. 2000. *T.S. Eliot—Poetry, Plays and Prose*. New Delhi: Atlantic Publishers & Distributors (P) Ltd. 168.

40. Kenner, Hugh. 1965. *The Invisible Poet: T.S. Eliot*. University Paperbacks. London: Metheun & Co. Ltd. 244.
41. Sarkar, Subhas. 2006. *T.S. Eliot—The Dramatist*. New Delhi: Atlantic Publishers & Distributors (P) Ltd. 102.
42. Singh, Parwati. 1988. *Character and Symbol in the Plays of T.S. Eliot*. New Delhi: Capital Publishing House. 31.
43. *Ibid*. 32-33.
44. Jones, D.E. 1960. *The Plays of T.S. Eliot*. London: Routledge & Kegan Paul. 50.
45. Singh, Parwati. 1988. *Character and Symbol in the Plays of T.S. Eliot*. New Delhi: Capital Publishing House. 32.
46. *Ibid*. 33.
47. Eliot, T.S. 1969. *The Complete Poems and Plays of T.S. Eliot*. London: Faber and Faber. 239.
48. *Ibid*.
49. *Ibid*. 281.
50. *Ibid*. 244.
51. *Ibid*. 243.
52. *Ibid*. 240.
53. *Ibid*.
54. *Ibid*. 243.
55. *Ibid*. 245.
56. *Ibid*. 256.
57. *Ibid*. 257.
58. *Ibid*. 258.
59. *Ibid*. 270.
60. *Ibid*.
61. *Ibid*. 272.
62. *Ibid*. 276.
63. *Ibid*. 272.
64. *Ibid*. 282.
65. Brooks, Cleanth. 1955. *Tragic Themes in Western Literature*. New Haven: Yale University Press. 170. Quoted in Sarkar, Subhas. 2006. *T.S. Eliot—The Dramatist*. New Delhi: Atlantic Publishers & Distributors (P) Ltd. 105.
66. Gardner, Helen. 1949. *The Art of T.S. Eliot*. London: The Cresset Press. 139. Quoted in Sarkar, Subhas. 2006. *T.S. Eliot—The*

Dramatist. New Delhi: Atlantic Publishers & Distributors (P) Ltd. 105.

67. Sarkar, Subhas. 2006. *T.S. Eliot—The Dramatist.* New Delhi: Atlantic Publishers & Distributors (P) Ltd. 107.
68. Kenner, Hugh. 1965. *The Invisible Poet: T.S. Eliot.* University Paperbacks. London: Metheun & Co. Ltd. 160.
69. Eliot, T.S. 1969. *The Complete Poems and Plays of T.S. Eliot.* London: Faber and Faber. 240.
70. Eliot, T.S. 1936. *The Need for Poetic Drama.* The Listener, November 25, 995. Quoted in Varshney, R.L. (Ed.). *T.S. Eliot's Murder in the Cathedral.* Agra: Laxmi Narain Agrawal. 98.
71. Jones, D.E. 1960. *The Plays of T.S. Eliot.* London: Routledge & Kegan Paul. 52-53.
72. *Ibid.* 53.
73. Eliot, T.S. 1969. *The Complete Poems and Plays of T.S. Eliot.* London: Faber and Faber. 239.
74. *Ibid.* 282.
75. *Ibid.* 240.
76. *Ibid.* 270.
77. *Ibid.* 282.
78. Raymond, Williams. 1954. *From Ibson to Eliot.* London: Chatto & Windus. 228.
79. Reynold, Peacock. 1946. *The Poet in the Theatre.* London: Routledge & Kegan Paul. 4. Quoted in Jones, D.E. 1960. *The Plays of T.S. Eliot.* London: Routledge & Kegan Paul. 57.
80. Jones, D.E. 1960. *The Plays of T.S. Eliot.* London: Routledge & Kegan Paul. 58.
81. Sarkar, Subhas. 2006. *T.S. Eliot—The Dramatist.* New Delhi: Atlantic Publishers & Distributors (P) Ltd. 97.
82. *Ibid.* 95-96.
83. Varshney, R.L. (Ed.). *T.S. Eliot's Murder in the Cathedral.* Agra: Laxmi Narain Agrawal. 99.
84. *Ibid.*
85. Gardner, Helen. 1949. *The Art of T.S. Eliot.* London: The Cresset Press. 136. Quoted in Sarkar, Subhas. 2006. *T.S. Eliot—The Dramatist.* New Delhi: Atlantic Publishers & Distributors (P) Ltd. 108.
86. Mathiessen, F.O. 1959. *The Achievement of T.S. Eliot.* New York: Oxford University Press. 162.

87. Eliot, T.S. 1950. *Poetry and Drama*. The Theodore Spencer Memorial Lecture, Harward University. Nov. 21, 1950. London: Faber and Faber.
88. Methuen's Study-Aid. 1971. *Notes on* T.S. Eliot's Murder in the Cathedral. London: Metheun & Co. Ltd. 35.
89. Sarkar, Subhas. 2006. *T.S. Eliot—The Dramatist*. New Delhi: Atlantic Publishers & Distributors (P) Ltd. 119.
90. Smith, Grover. 2000. *T.S. Eliot's Poetry and Plays*. Chicago: The University of Chicago Press. First Indian Reprint. Delhi: Doaba Publications. 193.
91. Eliot, T.S. 1969. *The Complete Poems and Plays of T.S. Eliot*. London: Faber and Faber. 245.
92. Henn, T.R. 1956. *The Harvest of Tragedy*. London: Methuen & Co. Ltd. 221.
93. Varshney, R.L. (Ed.). *T.S. Eliot's Murder in the Cathedral*. Agra: Laxmi Narain Agrawal. 103.
94. *Ibid*.

4

The Family Reunion

The Family Reunion is a play of sin and expiation. Eliot reflects, in this play, upon the absurdities of life and dramatizes the struggle of a penitent to cross the boundary line of the filthy world of disbelief and enter into 'the rose garden' of his soul's dream. While *Murder in the Cathedral* depicts the spiritual life and quest of a saint, *The Family Reunion* dramatizes the spiritual rebirth of an ordinary man, who is one of 'us.' It is one of the finest plays in the drawing room convention.

"In *The Family Reunion* Eliot chose the framework of a drawing room comedy for developing a theme that recalled the plays of Aeschylus. He took the theme of Orestes avenging his father's death by killing his mother from Aeschylus's 'Choephoroe', transformed the Furies into the Eumenides and gave a Christian colouring to the story.... Eliot takes up a similar theme of a curse which is inherited by the children from the parents and which they do their best to expiate."[1] "Unlike Orestes, he does not murder her (his mother) but he becomes nonetheless the instrument of her death."[2] "In ways both superficial and profound, Eliot presents himself as an adherent of classicism. This play strictly observes the unities of time and place. The traditional themes of ancient plays, sin and expiation, are used. A chorus and ghosts, 'invisible pursuers,' comply with classical precedents in tragedy. Both as an artist and as a thinker Eliot is very close to the classical tragedy."[3]

In *The Family Reunion* Eliot has endeavoured to present the drama of modern life in the framework of ritual. The two-fold elements of Greek and Christian rituals lie hidden in the structure of the play. Christian ritual of sin and redemption, however, supplies the scaffold of the drama. Eliot uses the Greek myth of the Oresteia as the fabric of its plot and designs it as "a crypto Christian play, with unfamiliar spiritual symbols and pagan overtones."[4] In this play Eliot has resolved the two-fold elements of pagan (Greek) and Christian rituals under the shadow of the Greek myth.

The play shows us a three-hour crisis in the life of Harry, Lord Monchensey. But this crisis has been brewing for the last forty years. We see Harry Monchensey at an earlier stage in his spiritual development when we meet him in the Family Reunion; for here we are not witnessing martyrdom but a conversion. He is in the throes of it as he arrives, hounded by guilt. At Wishwood he catches a glimpse of a long-lost innocent happiness in his talk with Mary, and of a life of self-denying love in his talk with Agatha. So to understand it, we must know what happened in those years. As it is impossible to reach the deeper meanings of Eliot's work without a clear knowledge of the story, it seems simplest to begin by gathering all the scattered hints and items of information together into a straightforward narrative. This information is gradually slipped out, here and there, during the play, but it is done so skilfully that we hardly notice we are being informed.

The curtain rises on a family, not fully assembled, to celebrate the 60th birthday of Amy, Dowager Lady Monchensey, at 'Wishwood', the family's country seat in the north of England, which according to Agatha 'was always a cold place.'[5] The name 'Wishwood' is symbolic, and "is intended by Eliot to stand for universal man's Dream House, located in a wood of wish and memory—turned to by man for refuge but discovered to be only an asylum for ghosts."[6] Amy has dominated it for nearly forty years, since her marriage to the late Lord Monchensey. It was a loveless marriage and had bred only unhappiness and evil. Although for a while the couple lived uneasily together at Wishwood, cold and lonely, and we are told, "there was no ecstasy."[7] For about three years the marriage hung fire and Amy, who was a natural matriarch, gradually transferred her feeling of possession from her husband to Wishwood itself, her new home.

"And reached the point where
Wishwood supported her, and she supported Wishwood."[8]

The husband was mildly continuing to lead a rather withdrawn, sensitive inward life.

He had his strength beneath unusual weakness,
The diffidence of a solitary man:
Where he was weak, he recognized his wife's power
And yielded to it.[9]

Thus, although Amy was gathering strength, both still felt very lonely:

A man and a woman
Married, alone in a lonely country house together,
For three years childless, learning the meaning
Of loneliness.[10]

So Amy felt that if she was to become a matriarch, she must first coldly see to it that she becomes a mother.

I would have sons, if I could not have a husband:[11]

While Amy was in her first pregnancy, Amy's younger sister, Agatha then a girl of twenty-one and still at college came to spend her vacation at Wishwood and at once fell in love with her brother-in-law, and he with her

I only looked through the little door
When the sun was shining on the rose-garden
And heard in the distance the tiny voices
And then a black raven flew over.[12]

Then Autumn came and Amy's child—Harry that was to be—was due before Christmas. But the unwilling father on whom she had forced this son was already trying to think (but with no success) how to murder his wife.

I found him thinking
How to get rid of your mother. What simple plots!
He was not suited to the role of murderer[13]

But Agatha restrained him from such foolish fantasies. Agatha was also thinking of her sister's child to be, with whom she had developed a secret bond of affinity. She wished, it had been her child and loved it as if it were. The love she felt for Harry's father was spiritually transferred to Harry. But Agatha and Harry's father knew that they must part, who had never actually been truly together. They were to turn away from each other; she to walk endlessly "down a concrete corridor, in a dead air."[14] However, "there was never the slightest suspicion of scandal."[15] In due course Harry was born and in the years that followed his brothers—John and Arthur—were born too. After seven years of this 'life in death,' with uncommitted murder in his heart, Amy's husband left her,

"Seven years I kept him,
For the sake of the future, a discontented ghost.
In his own house."[16]

He, then, travelled abroad and faded out in solitude. We are told nothing about his death save that he died when Harry was still a boy.[17] Meanwhile, Agatha, having renounced her love, returned to her academic life, accepted her spinsterhood, and gave her great talent to the government of a woman's college. Thus both the sisters were governing two different institutions. Agatha governed a College, Amy her family at Wishwood.

Amy's thoughts were now devoted to the future of Wishwood and she felt that Harry must marry. So she picked up Mary, a remote cousin of her own—a young and submissive girl and imported her to Wishwood for her holidays, "She only wanted to have a tame daughter-in-law with very little money, a housekeeper-companion for her and Harry."[18] Mary, however, fell quietly and permanently in love with Harry as Amy had intended, but unfortunately Harry had no such feeling for her. So Mary, even though unwanted, remained a permanent guest in the great, cold, hate-filled house.

The oppression of Wishwood and its matriarch was increasingly felt by Harry during his school years. He had never known affectionate love. And through these loveless years, Harry rose to manhood and felt the need for independence. He chose a wife of the kind who could cut him adrift from Wishwood, as Amy diagnosed the motive of her son's ill chosen wife:

She never wished to be one of the family,
She only wanted to keep him to herself
To satisfy her vanity.[19]

The marriage was as loveless as his father's had been. The pattern was still imprecise, but the new loneliness was there, just as it had been when Harry's father had married Amy. Harry tells Agatha of his feelings at that time:

> At the beginning, eight years ago
> I felt, at first that sense of separation,
> Of isolation unredeemable, irrevocable—[20]

History was beginning to repeat itself. Harry, escaping from the possessive tyrannous love of his mother, accepted a separation from Wishwood but his wife also could not give him the much needed love. His father's curse was being revisited on him. He also began to dream of a murder as his father had been dreaming of murdering Amy—'simple plots.' He was not 'suited to the role of murderer' either. A kind of numbness or starvation settled upon him and the sense of being in a dream or nightmare, which seemed to be the curse upon his father was beginning to operate on him. He had strange fancies, and a strange way of expressing them as if he were a poet:

> "Perhaps my life has only been a dream
> Dreamt through me by the minds of others"[21]

For eight years of constant attendance on an estranging marriage, that led him from party to party, country to country and continent to continent, high on the heals of his wife, the nightmare gathered strength, until at last, the 'murder' happened. Harry's wife, by one account, was "swept off the deck in the middle of a storm."[22] But by Harry's account, "he pushed her overboard on a cloudless night in the mid-Atlantic."[23] Although he later realized, "Perhaps I only dreamt I pushed her,"[24] but if it was a dream, it was a dream of wishfulfilment. As uncle Charles says, "I suspect it is simply the wish to get rid of her/ Makes him believe he did."[25] The guilt of the wish haunted him as he had committed the murder at least in his heart. Such at least was his nightmarish impression of events.

It was from that confused moment that he began to feel himself haunted and hunted by seemingly evil supernatural presences that remained invisible—the Eumenides. So to escape from them his instinct brought him home. But where he had gone to seek safety, the 'sleepless hunters' had already reached before him and there they suddenly appear and confront him. It was his mother's birthday, when he reaches home and finds his family assembled and waiting for him. It is here that the play begins.

The play opens with a portrait of Wishwood, the dead end of an old family, where different members have gathered without any affection, simply in obedience to Amy. Into that little world of his mother's self-centeredness, Harry storms in, seemingly mad, pursued by the Eumenides. For the first time he sees them in Wishwood, though they had been chasing him everywhere since long. But then, "Why should they wait until I came to Wishwood?"[26] Harry, however, cannot explain his agony, more so to his uncles and aunts "to whom nothing has happened."[27] Harry, on the other hand, is wading through the nightmarish dark night of his soul, burning in purgatorial flames. Like Hamlet, he finds it impossible to put the world in order.

The second scene of Part I begins with a conversation between Mary and Agatha. Once it was decided that Mary and Harry would enter into marriage lock, but it did not happen. So Agatha consoles and advises Mary to wait, "You and I, Mary,/ Are only watchers and waiters: not the easiest role."[28] As Agatha leaves Harry enters and Harry and Mary talk about their childhood memories and at the end of the scene Eumenides the unseen powers appear before Harry, but Mary doesn't see them.

Then the third scene of Part I opens with Harry, Mary, Ivy, Violet, Gerald and Charles on the stage. Dinner is getting ready, while Dr. Warburton, 'the oldest friend of the family'[29] also arrives. While all of them talk about ordinary matters, Harry speaks of the presentness of the past and says that, "past is unredeemable."[30] In the meanwhile, both the Chorus and Agatha perceive premonition. The Chorus sings, "I am afraid of all that has happened, and all that is to come"[31] and Agatha thinks that some evil spirit has settled on the house:

"The eye of the day time
And the eye of the night time

Be diverted from this house
Till the knot is unknotted
The crossed is uncrossed
And the crooked is made straight."[32]

Then the first scene of Part II begins with Harry and Warburton in the library after dinner. Warburton advises Harry to look after his mother's future happiness. He says that Amy is very ill and that, "it is only the force of her personality,/ Her indomitable will, that keeps her alive."[33] Then Denman enters and informs that Sergeant Winchell has come with the news that Harry's brother John "had a bit of an accident."[34] Although Harry remains unperturbed, all others are afraid of something ominous. The Chorus sings:

"And whatever happens began in the past, and presses hard on the future
The agony in the curtained bedroom, whether of birth or of dying
Gathers in to itself all the voices of the past and projects them into the future"[35]

The second scene of Part II begins with Harry's recanting his wretchedness, his apprehensions of the unseen powers (the Furies), and his philosophy of eternity and describes the nature of his 'free floating fear of the Furies.' Then on Harry's demand Agatha narrates the history of his mother and father, and how lonely they felt together. Agatha also tells how she fell in love with his father and he with her. Agatha also told that Harry's father wanted to get rid of Amy and Agatha restrained him from that crime because she felt an affinity for Harry as if he was her own son. So now, Harry is suffering because he has to expatiate the sin of his father. Harry gradually passes from his casual interest in commonplace events to an understanding of the spiritual reality, in which this physical world of events appears as 'unreal' and 'unimportant.' He moves further towards progressive realization of his spiritual choice. So when Eumenides appear again before Harry, he is not afraid of them and takes a decision of renunciation. The Furies, at first, haunted Harry like the fateful spirit of revenge, but towards the end of the play appear as 'the bright angels' whom he would gladly follow. As Harry himself says:

"...this is the first time that I have been free
From the ring of ghosts with joined hands, from the pursuers,
And come into a quiet place."[36]

Similarly, Agatha also takes the place of the Eumenides because she is Harry's spiritual guide or guardian. So as Amy arrives Harry informs her of his decision to leave Wishwood and to "follow the bright angels."[37]

Then as the third scene of Part II begins, Amy accuses Agatha of taking away her husband, thirty-five years ago and now she accuses Agatha of taking away her son too:

Thirty-five years ago
You took my husband from me. Now you take my son.[38]

Then Mary also enters and requests Agatha to stop Harry from going away from Wishwood. But Agatha tells them that, "Harry has crossed the frontier/ Beyond which safety and danger have a different meaning./ And he cannot return."[39] Just then Harry enters for departure and tells his mother that she has nothing to worry about Arthur and John and himself, and bids goodbye to all. Amy also realizes her mistakes and says, "I always wanted too much for my children/ More than life can give. And now I am punished for it."[40] She leaves to the next room for rest and after a short while we hear her final voice "Agatha! Mary! Come!/ The clock has stopped in the dark!"[41] Amy thus collapses with Harry's departure. "But her death is symbolic of the end of the closed world of loveless existence."[42] The Chorus helplessly sings: "We have lost our way in the dark."[43] The play ends with Agatha's closing words, which form the Epilogue of the play:

"This way the pilgrimage
Of expiation
Round and round the circle
Completing the charm
So the knot be unknotted
The crossed be uncrossed

The crocked be made straight
And the curse be ended
By intercession
By pilgrimage
By those who depart
In several directions
For their own redemption
And that of the departed—
May they rest in peace."[44]

Helen Gardner offers an interesting interpretation of the play's ending: "No answer is given or can be given to Amy's question: 'Why are you going?' or the other question: 'Where are you going?' The audience is no wiser than the Chorus. We can use psychological terms and say that Harry's departure is an act by which he expresses the end of his mother's fixation. We can use religious terms and say that Harry's departure expresses his discovery that his obligation is not to his mother, but to God; that he is one of those who are called to 'leave all and follow.' Neither conception gives us a true ending of a play.... At the heart of the play is the Christian doctrine of Atonement, and the mysterious exchange of sin and suffering in the spiritual world through which mankind partakes in that mystery. This call Harry perceives and he leaves to follow it. Whether he will fulfil his calling, or how—we do not know. His exit is not an end but a beginning."[45]

To put the essence of action briefly, we can say that, "Harry returns, guilty of murder in his heart, to Wishwood, in hysterical flight from the avenging angels of conscience; but thanks to his conversations, first with Marry and later with Agatha, his heart is changed and he comes to understand that he must follow these angels, however great the suffering it may involve, and not flee from. That change of heart is the action of the play."[46]

Like *Murder in the Cathedral*, this play also deals with the choice of the hero between a mundane order and a spiritual one. The opposite poles are incarnated in the persons of Harry and Amy. They voice the two opposing forces, the moment of whose collusion creates the situation of the play. Amy, the widowed mother of Harry, "bears a close resemblance to Lord Claverton of *The Elder Statesman*, who suffers from the same sense of alienation from the warmth of life and love because of his possessive instinct."[47] Harry represents Consciousness rising to its spiritual level. The clash between Harry and Amy, Consciousness and the Earthly order occasion the central situation of the play. The symbol of the earthly order is the clock, whose regular ticking is a certainty of the continuity of life. "Amy lives in a pattern of timed moments, by the clock; like the works of a clock she is a machine."[48] It is this mission, which keeps Amy tied down to Wishwood:

"I do not want the clock to stop in the dark
If you want to know why I never leave Wishwood
This is the reason, I keep Wishwood alive
To keep the family alive, to keep them together,
To keep me alive, and I live to keep them."[49]

Harry on his part endeavours to communicate his experience to them but finds words inadequate. He, therefore, tries to speak in parables and analogies. Harry found in his life a sense of happiness, which descended upon him after having undergone great inner spiritual struggle. His sense of guilt and the urge for expiation has helped him to discover the true glory and vision of life.

Harry, who is a child born of animal passion rather than of human love, develops an awareness of the predicament of the sinful man. His sense of guilt haunts him like a curse. "The Furies appear before him twice, once in the presence of his cousin Mary who was to have been his wife and again in the presence of his aunt Agatha. The first scene, Eliot himself said, is symbolic of Harry's attraction-repulsion complex about Mary and as for the second; he finds a refuge in an ambiguous relation—the attraction, half of a son and half of a lover, to Agatha. They are the people who bring him news 'of a door that opens at the end of a corridor.'"[50] But Agatha, the most potent spiritual agent guides Harry not to move towards 'evasion of suffering' but by untying the knot and moving ahead in the pursuit of liberation. Bound to the rim of the wheel of purgatorial fire, and wishing to leap forward towards the still centre, the process of expiation begins till Harry gains 'a different vision':

> "Now I see
> I have been wounded in a war of phantoms.
> Not by human beings—they have no more power than I
> The things I thought real are shadows, and the real
> Are what I thought were private shadows."[51]

Agatha further guides him towards the vision of Eden—the vision of 'the rose garden,' but warns him that he has to embark on a long journey and instead of running away from the Eumenides, he 'must follow the bright angels.'[52] Thus Harry is 'crossing the frontiers'[53] and getting rid of the world of 'birth and life'[54] after passing through the purgatorial agony of renunciation and having a glimpse of the paradisal experience of the Eternal, but as to when the vision of "the rose-garden"[55] or of a "shaft of sunlight"[56] may appear, he cannot premeditate:

> "One thing you cannot know
> The sudden extinction of every alternative
> The unexpected crash of the iron cataract."[57]

Mary also consoles him and reveals that:

> "I believe the moment of birth
> Is when we have knowledge of death
> I believe the season of birth
> Is the season of sacrifice."[58]

As the clock of Amy stops in the dark[59] and as the chorus of uninitiated ignorant men and women realize, "We have lost our ways in the dark."[60] Harry moved on the way of his pilgrimage of expiation, where the knot may be unknotted, the crooked made straight,[61] the curse ended and they rest in peace. Thus Agatha's summary of the play's Climax is intended to express the symbolic meaning of the events portrayed in the play:

> "What we have written is not a story of detection,
> Of crime and punishment, but of sin and expiation"[62]

"In the conflict between two realms of existence represented by Amy and Harry, the role of the chorus is to show, first by their unwilling acceptance of membership in Amy's cast of characters, then by their gradual confusion at the disruption of the events they expected to occur, and finally by their fear and glimmering awareness, the gradual victory of the eternal over the temporal."[63] The Chorus of Uncles and Aunts symbolizes worldly people "who stand here like guilty conspirators waiting for some revelation/ When the hidden shall be exposed."[64] They express their state of bewilderment about the chain of events which they cannot comprehend.

"These choral characters have hardly any distinct individuality of their own. However, in specific moments, they have partial access into the spiritual realm—something akin to hints and guesses, as experienced by the dwellers of the time-ridden world of Four Quartets."[65] "In *The Family Reunion* some of the minor characters themselves give up their individual roles in the play to speak collectively as Chorus."[66]

On the other hand, Dr. Warburton, Mary and Agatha are the spiritually enlightened. Thus the characters in *The Family Reunion* also can be classified into three groups. Amy represents the *Blind*, Dr. Warburton, Mary and Agatha the *Helpers* and Harry is the *Seeker*. "Agatha, Harry's aunt plays the same role that Monica does in *The Elder Statesman* and that Sir Henry Harcourt Reilly plays in *The Cocktail Party*."[67] "In *The Family Reunion* there are three characters who see the Eumenides, apart from Harry. They are Agatha, Mary and Downing. All the three of them are themselves not in the same class as Harry, but each in his way helps Harry to make the right choice and contribute to the ultimate result."[68]

"Agatha is the priestess-sybil of *The Family Reunion*, with an humble assistant in Mary. Their function appears to be psycho-therapeutic; to induce Harry to reveal himself to himself, to accept the Recognition through the appearance of Furies; as the curious trinity of Reilly, Julia and Alex determine the destinies of the other characters in *The Cocktail Party*."[69]

"There is undoubtedly a gap between the two different levels of understanding: of Agatha, Mary and Harry on the one hand and the rest of the characters on the other.... These two planes of existence, correspond to Eliot's design of poetic play which offers an element of ambivalence or duality of the pattern of life.... Between these two levels of understanding, Downing provides the missing link.... Downing, undoubtedly, acts as the bridge between the two different planes of existence or sensibility as represented by the two contrasting groups of characters."[70] Besides Amy who persuades Harry to take up the role of running the House of Wishwood, Mary and Dr. Warburton also in a way play the role of tempters in *The Family Reunion*. Mary tempts Harry with her limited and selfish love, which is distinct from spiritual or ecstatic love, and Dr. Warburton tries to dissuade Harry from his spiritual quest by rousing in him a sense of pity for his mother. But, "Agatha, like his guardian angel, constantly guards him against worldly temptations.... Like the subsidiary Chorus, she now and again throws hints and suggestions about the important characters of the play. Without Agatha we would hardly understand Harry's past and its relevance to the present or the future."[71]

According to Ronald Peacock,[72] these 'moments are the projections of the unheard and unspoken life that flows through *The Family Reunion*.' Whenever Eliot introduces one or the other character, it is in the individual voice like the 'aside' that predominates. But their joint utterances in the totality represent the 'general or the universal attitude of the common people.'

Thus Eliot, in this play, has shown some rethinking in the use of the chorus. Perhaps, he realized that, in *Murder in the Cathedral*, he depended heavily on the assistance of the chorus. Therefore, he decided to integrate chorus more closely into the play. As a result he tried to dispense with the chorus in *The Family Reunion* but did not altogether abandon its use. Instead, he retained its role and restricted the number of choric speeches to four; individualized its members; and assigned them roles quite independent of their collective character. According to Frederic Lumley, "the experiment of using, as Chorus, four minor characters whose sudden ritualistic chant seems quite out of harmony and their previous roles can only be described as embarrassing."[73]

Eliot himself regards the device as 'very unsatisfactory,' since it creates problems for the actors. It also obstructs the proper growth of the action. The major hurdle in this connection arises out of an immediate transition from individual characterized part to members of the chorus. "It is," says Eliot, "a very difficult transition to accomplish."[74]

In the first scene, the choric figures cling to their physical sense of reality apprehending a vague sense of fear and anxiety like the chorus in *Murder in the Cathedral*. Just before Harry enters, they voice their unease at being assembled "at Amy's command to play an unread part in some monstrous farce, ridiculous in some nightmare pantomime."[75] When Harry told that he had pushed his wife over board and Downing had seemed to corroborate this, they are assailed by the fear of a public scandal and terror of the ugly reality that may be revealed, which they would prefer to ignore. It is not nice to have a murderer in the family, but it's worse still to realize that the unknown has irrupted into the family circle and that you no longer recognize your nephew. For the chorus:

"Any explanation will satisfy;
We only ask to be reassured
About the noises in the cellar
And the window that should not have been open.
Why do we all behave as if the door might suddenly open, the curtains be drawn,
The cellar make some dreadful disclosure, the roof disappear,
And we should cease to be sure of what is real or unreal
Hold tight, hold tight, we must insist that the world is what we have taken it be."[76]

"Towards the close of the first scene in Part I the chorus voices the general feeling of unrest which arises out of their difficulty of understanding the spiritual drama in which they are 'implicated' and as it disintegrates into individual voices of Ivy, Violet and Charles, the limitations of different individuals are pronounced by one another.... Ronald Peacock characterizes this new form of the chorus as the 'formalized extension' of the 'aside.' It has high formal value, as this new treatment of the classical convention attains its goal without making it artificial."[77]

The chorus is significantly absent in the second scene of the play. Here, evidently the dramatist's intention is to focus attention on the development of Harry, the quester. "There are

The Family Reunion

two lyrical duets in the play, between Harry and Mary and Harry and Agatha, which are in a sense 'beyond character' for they reach the level of expressionistic drama of a kind of 'poetic fantasia.'"[78]

In the third scene of Part I, the chorus reappears. They strike a note of fear, which emanates from a feeling of moral responsibility, clearly outside the domain of common people. They dread being drawn into something different from ordinary reality. They are afraid because their comfortable conception of time as an orderly succession is threatened and their complacent picture of family history as a series of innocent snapshots imperilled:

> "And the wings of the future darken the past, the beak and claws have desecrated
> History shamed
> The first cry in the bedroom, the noise in the nursery, mutilated
> The family album, rendered ludicrous
> The tenants' dinner, the family picnic on the Moors."[79]

Then in the first scene of Part II, they again express their apprehensions about the possibility of a curse on the house. The chorus speaks of the inherited sense of agony and the deception of keeping up appearances in the face of certain inflexible laws.

> "In an old house there is always listening, and more is heard than is spoken
> And what is spoken remains in the room, waiting for the future to hear it.
> And whatever happens began in the past, and presses hard on the future
> The agony in the curtained bedroom, whether of birth or of dying
> Gathers in to itself all the voices of the past, and projects them into the future."[80]

But they evade the implications. They conclude that 'there is nothing at all to be done about it, and turn their attention to the weather and the 'international catastrophes'[81] the distant evils about which they cannot do anything. They recoil from what they do not understand, from the great unanswered questions about ultimate reality, and take refuge in the pseudo-realities of social convention: "We must adjust ourselves to the moment: we must do the right thing."[82] These choric utterances are an explicit statement of the common people's sense of limited knowledge and their apprehension of something happening beyond the circle of understanding. It may be fair to surmise that each character in the play feels as the chorus do, that he is 'playing the unreal part' in some other character's play. The final chorus at the end of scene III of Part II expresses a sense of bafflement, but at the same time recognizes, the inability to understand the situation. The more we know, the more conscious we become of our ignorance. The choric speech points to the impossibility of communication and understanding, which is part of the human situation.

Thus as Subhas Sarkar says, Eliot's "true greatness lies in skilful handling of poetry as the proper medium for his drawing-room play. Discarding the conventional blank verse for his poetic drama he has created a verse-form which incorporates all kinds of contemporary speech ranging from banal drawing room conversation to the serious and reflective talks revealing the height of the emotional and spiritual reality."[83]

Eliot evolved a very flexible verse form in *The Family Reunion*, which he was to use in his other plays as well. He has used "a line of varying length and varying number of syllables, with a caesura and three stresses, with one stress on one side of the caesura and two on the other.... The flexible line evolved by Eliot is capable of expressing the widest range of feeling and the most varied kind of experiences. The stiffness of Charles's character is indicated by the heavy rhythm of the verse used by him, the more complex character of Gerald by a relaxed but convoluted verse, the jerky movements suggests the tension in Mary's mind and the repetitions which bind together Amy's speeches indicate her dominating character. The combination of the conversational tone with the haunting rhythm of some of Harry's speeches suggests how his mind can jump from the plane of the real to that of the mystical."[84] "Verse of this kind specializes the play considerably; for while it adds an extra-dimension to the drawing room realities, it throws the responsibility for this dimension upon the language alone."[85]

D.E. Jones also gives a valuable analysis of the verse patterns of the choral characters in *The Plays of T.S. Eliot*, "The degree of control that the verse gives over characterization and dramatic tension can be illustrated from the scene in which the uncles and aunts discuss 'the younger generation'.... Here, the stiff, pompous, insensitive rhythm which characterizes Charles, especially in his more obtuse mood, gives way to an ampler, more relaxed, but still circumscribed movement as Gerald makes his kindly gesture. Mary's pent up emotion reveals itself in a very jerky movement (the repetitions in 'information...generation' and 'I don't deserve.... I don't belong' are the more obvious means of achieving a kind of stumbling bitterness). The awkward silence, which covers her exit, is broken by Violet's sharp decisiveness. Gerald's reaction does not go deeper than bemusement; the rhythm has only a slight hesitancy. With his stolid complacency, Charles moves firmly in, to put Mary's outburst into perspective, as he would think. And, finally, Amy with her characteristically domineering rhythm closes the incident. The tenacious rhythm of her monosyllabic half-line 'but life still go right' prevents us from interpreting it as mere wish; she clearly intends to do what she can, to make it go right. The scene demonstrates that poetic drama can have something of the precision of a musical score. Character and dramatic structure are here integrated in the verse rhythm, through which the tension of the awkward moment is built-up and resolved."[86]

Thus, "In *The Family Reunion*, Eliot has tried to integrate the chorus closely into the central design of the play. He has, however, chosen to limit it to the expression of sterile fear and baffled understanding and thereby, he has run the risk of lowering the dramatic temperature. Unlike the tremendous emotional release provided in *Murder in the Cathdral*, the chorus in *The Family Reunion* has a limited role to play."[87]

"If the chorus is meant to represent something like the ordinary level of insight—or rather lack of insight—and to be the means by which the average member of an audience is enabled to penetrate to the deeper level at which the essential action proceeds, then one must conclude that the gap between the two levels is too wide. Of course one will identify oneself entirely with the slightly caricatured uncles and aunts, but even if one starts ahead of them the territory soon becomes too strange for most people.... For this reason *The Family Reunion* is not likely to appeal to an average audience, and if Eliot meant it merely for special audiences, there would be no end of the matter."[88]

The quartet of uncles and aunts who compose the chorus, seem with one partial exception, to be unable to understand what is happening; Charles alone has a glimmering of its significance:

"It's very odd,
But I am beginning to feel, just beginning to feel
That there is something, I *could* understand, if I were told it."[89]

"But most of the time he is like the others, a representative of obtuse humanity. They are stock English types, slightly caricatured. From time to time they draw together, as if to find safety in numbers and voice their fear of the Unknown."[90]

As Mathiessen points out, "They are unlike the usual Greek chorus in that, their role is not to illuminate the action but to express the baffled inability to understand what is happening"[91] because, however, they express small everyday fears which members of the audience will recognize akin to their own experience. They form a link between the audience and the action. The difficulty of the play stems from the fact that Harry's experience is exceptional and remote. At a level of apprehension nearer that of an average member of an audience, the Chorus expresses the fear of spiritual reality, which Harry comes to accept. By implication, therefore, they help to interpret the action, even though they do not understand it.

As Carol H. Smith says, "The function of the chorus as a reactor to and reflector of the dramatic action is pointed up in *The Family Reunion* by the use of theatrical imagery by chorus members Ivy, Violet, Gerald, and Charles. They continually see themselves as unwillingly playing parts assigned to them by

Amy. The kinship with Amy and with her husband indicates that they are meant to represent the 'type of the common man' which might, but usually does not, perceive the spiritual dimension of life."[92]

But, however, Eliot in *The Family Reunion* tries to make the chorus more relevant to everyday experience of the audience. He tries to win over the audience to a new way of life. Even the chorus follows the same pattern. It is closely integrated into the play. It consists of Harry's uncles and aunts but its role is essentially different from that usually assigned to the Greek chorus. It is no more there in its conventional sense of 'illuminating the action'. On the other hand it creates a relative feeling of inability to discern what is happening on the stage.

Commenting on the character of the chorus in *The Family Reunion*, Carol H. Smith says, "In *The Family Reunion* the chorus is made up of individual members of Harry's family who, though they remain relatively flat characters, are individualized by their differing reactions to the hero's dilemma and by the characteristic verse patterns each is given to speak. Since in this play, Eliot was still trying for the stylized effect of Ben Jonson's flat characters, these characters are left undeveloped intentionally in order that they may fulfil their function in the microcosmic dramatic world."[93]

The chorus in *The Family Reunion*, as a whole is not so successful. Eliot became aware that he had depended heavily on the chorus in *Murder in the Cathedral* and decided that next time he would "try to integrate the chorus more closely into the play."[94] Therefore, he has reduced that number of his chorus to four and individualized its members, giving functions and characteristics independent of its choric functions. But this involves a number of difficulties. He himself now considers the device unsatisfactory because of the problem it presents to the actor, the problem of transition "from individual characterized part to membership of a chorus."[95]

Thus Raymond Williams has rightly said that, "The Chorus of *The Family Reunion* had not been very satisfactory; the verse was adequate, but the formal convention depended upon a sudden change of function by the aunts and uncles, who had been set in a deliberate comic characterization and were required suddenly to become agents of a formal community; this was not easy to accept."[96]

In conclusion, one may say that there exists a virtual consort between Eliot's method and matter. It initiates a process of conflict, tension and conciliation. Since they involve various states of the mind, their precise presentation in the drama becomes all the more difficult. His major achievement, therefore, is the way he has developed appropriate methods to integrate the subject matter of his theme with dramatic structure of his play. "Thus the chorus in *The Family Reunion* offers an excellent example of Eliot's successful adaptation of the classical convention to the modern realistic setting. Both in its form and application it has received an almost new dimension of meaning in the play. In his adaptation of the chorus to the requirements of the modern realistic setting in the play.... ...Eliot has undoubtedly offered a novel example of the synthesis of the classical and the naturalistic convention."[97]

NOTES AND REFERENCES

1. Chaturvedi, B.N. 1967. *English Poetic Drama of the Twentieth Century.* Gwalior: Kitab Ghar. 59.
2. Ibid. 62.
3. Gowda, Anniah. 1972. *The Revival of English Poetic Drama.* New Delhi: Orient Longman Ltd. 329-30.
4. Coghill, Nevill (Ed.). 1963. *T.S. Eliot's The Family Reunion.* Delhi: Oxford University Press. 13.
5. Eliot, T.S. 1969. *The Complete Poems and Plays of T.S. Eliot.* London: Faber and Faber. 285.
6. Smith, Carol H. 1963. *T.S. Eliot's Dramatic Theory and Practice.* London: Oxford University Press. 136n.
7. Eliot, T.S. 1969. *The Complete Poems and Plays of T.S. Eliot.* London: Faber and Faber. 332.
8. Ibid.
9. Ibid. 331-32.
10. Ibid. 332.
11. Ibid. 340.

12. *Ibid.* 334-35.
13. *Ibid.* 332.
14. *Ibid.* 335.
15. *Ibid.* 319.
16. *Ibid.* 340.
17. *Ibid.* 319.
18. *Ibid.* 304.
19. *Ibid.* 289-90.
20. *Ibid.* 330.
21. *Ibid.* 333.
22. *Ibid.* 289.
23. *Ibid.* 294.
24. *Ibid.* 333.
25. *Ibid.* 296.
26. *Ibid.* 292.
27. *Ibid.* 293.
28. *Ibid.* 305.
29. *Ibid.* 314.
30. *Ibid.* 315.
31. *Ibid.*
32. *Ibid.* 316.
33. *Ibid.* 320.
34. *Ibid.* 322.
35. *Ibid.* 329.
36. *Ibid.* 336.
37. *Ibid.* 339.
38. *Ibid.* 340.
39. *Ibid.* 342.
40. *Ibid.* 345.
41. *Ibid.* 347.
42. Sarkar, Subhas. 2006. *T.S. Eliot—The Dramatist.* New Delhi: Atlantic Publishers & Distributors (P) Ltd. 160.
43. Eliot, T.S. 1969. *The Complete Poems and Plays of T.S. Eliot.* London: Faber and Faber. 349.
44. *Ibid.* 350.

45. Gardner, Helen. 1949. *The Art of T.S. Eliot*. London: The Cresset Press. 155-56. Quoted in Sarkar, Subhas. 2006. *T.S. Eliot—The Dramatist*. New Delhi: Atlantic Publishers & Distributors (P) Ltd. 152.
46. Coghill, Nevill (Ed.). 1963. *T.S. Eliot's the Family Reunion*. Delhi: Oxford University Press. 29.
47. Sarkar, Subhas. 2006. *T.S. Eliot—The Dramatist*. New Delhi: Atlantic Publishers & Distributors (P) Ltd. 156.
48. Smith, Grover. 2000. *T.S. Eliot's Poetry and Plays—A Study in Sources and Meaning*. Chicago: The University of Chicago Press. First Indian Reprint. Delhi: Doaba Publications. 198.
49. Eliot, T.S. 1969. *The Complete Poems and Plays of T.S. Eliot*. London: Faber and Faber. 287.
50. Chaturvedi, B.N. 1967. *English Poetic Drama of the Twentieth Century*. Gwalior: Kitab Ghar. 59.
51. Eliot, T.S. 1969. *The Complete Poems and Plays of T.S. Eliot*. London: Faber and Faber. 334.
52. *Ibid*. 339.
53. *Ibid*. 342.
54. *Ibid*.
55. *Ibid*. 335.
56. *Ibid*.
57. *Ibid*. 307.
58. *Ibid*. 310.
59. *Ibid*. 347.
60. *Ibid*. 349.
61. *Ibid*. 350.
62. *Ibid*. 333.
63. Smith, Carol H. 1963. *T.S. Eliot's Dramatic Theory and Practice*. London: Oxford University Press. 146.
64. Eliot, T.S. 1969. *The Complete Poems and Plays of T.S. Eliot*. London: Faber and Faber. 301.
65. Singh, Parwati. 1988. *Character and Symbol in the Plays of T.S. Eliot*. Delhi: Capital Publishing House. 76.
66. Chaturvedi, B.N. 1967. *English Poetic Drama of the Twentieth Century*. Gwalior: Kitab Ghar. 61.
67. Sharma, Jitendra Kumar. 1985. *Time & T.S. Eliot*. New Delhi: Sterling Publishers Private Limited. 119.

68. Rampal, Dushiant Kumar. 1996. *Poetic Theory and Practice of T.S. Eliot*. New Delhi: Atlantic Publishers & Distributors (P) Ltd. 230.

69. Henn, T.R. 1956. *The Harvest of Tragedy*. London: Methuen & Co. Ltd. 225.

70. Sarkar, Subhas. 2006. *T.S. Eliot—The Dramatist*. New Delhi: Atlantic Publishers and Distributors (P) Ltd. 142-143.

71. *Ibid.* 161.

72. Peacock, Ronald. 1961. *The Poet in the Theatre*. London: Macgibbon & Kee. 16.

73. Lumley, Fredrick. *New Trends in Twentieth Century Drama*. 131. Quoted in Sharma, H.L. 1976. *T.S. Eliot—His Dramatic Theories*. New Delhi: S. Chand & Co. 80.

74. Eliot, T.S. 1957. *On Poetry and Poets*. London: Faber and Faber. 82.

75. Eliot, T.S. 1969. *The Complete Poems and Plays of T.S. Eliot*. London: Faber and Faber. 291.

76. *Ibid.* 302.

77. Sarkar, Subhas. 2006. *T.S. Eliot—The Dramatist*. New Delhi: Atlantic Publishers & Distributors. 162-63.

78. Chaturvedi, B.N. 1967. *English Poetic Drama of the Twentieth Century*. Gwalior: Kitab Ghar. 61.

79. Eliot, T.S. 1969. *The Complete Poems and Plays of T.S. Eliot*. London: Faber and Faber. 315.

80. *Ibid.* 328-29.

81. *Ibid.* 329.

82. *Ibid.* 349.

83. Sarkar, Subhas. 2006. *T.S. Eliot—The Dramatist*. New Delhi: Atlantic Publishers & Distributors (P) Ltd. 165.

84. Chaturvedi, B.N. 1967. *English Poetic Drama of the Twentieth Century*. Gwalior: Kitab Ghar. 82-83.

85. Kenner, Hugh. 1966. *The Invisible Poet—T.S. Eliot*. University Paperbacks. London: Metheun & Co. Ltd. 283.

86. Smith, Carol H. 1963. *T.S. Eliot's Dramatic Theory and Practice*. London: Oxford University Press. 119-20n.

87. Singh, Parwati. 1988. *Character and Symbol in the Plays of T.S. Eliot*. Delhi: Capital Publishing House. 77.

88. Jones, D.E. 1960. *The Plays of T.S. Eliot*. London: Routledge & Kegan Paul. 110.

89. Eliot, T.S. 1969. *The Complete Poems and Plays of T.S. Eliot.* London: Faber and Faber. 345.
90. Jones, D.E. 1960. *The Plays of T.S. Eliot.* London: Routledge & Kegan Paul. 106.
91. Methiessen, F.O. 1976. *The Achievement of T.S. Eliot.* London: Oxford University Press. 166.
92. Smith, Carol H. 1963. *T.S. Eliot's Dramatic Theory and Practice.* London: Oxford University Press. 145.
93. *Ibid.* 119-20.
94. Eliot, T.S. 1957. *On Poetry and Poets.* London: Faber and Faber. 81.
95. *Ibid.* 82.
96. Williams, Raymond. *Drama from Ibson to Eliot.* London: Chatto & Windus. 237.
97. Sarkar, Subhas. 2006. *T.S. Eliot—The Dramatist.* New Delhi: Atlantic Publishers & Distributors (P) Ltd. 165.

5

The Cocktail Party

The Cocktail Party was first staged in 1949 and was at once a great success. It was written for the Edinburgh Festival, but it had even greater success when staged in New York and London in 1950. The play in three Acts has been written in modern setting. It begins with a cocktail party and ends with another cocktail party. The play mainly deals with the conjugal disharmony, a problem that very much disturbs the modern societies. "In *The Cocktail Party*, then, Eliot depicts no human relationship which is satisfactory in itself. Those who think they love cannot marry; those who are married simply endure."[1] "The point of the comic situation of unreciprocated love—Lavinia in love with Peter, Peter in love with Celia, Celia in love with Edward, and Edward in love with himself"[2] presents a complex situation before the audience. While Edward is incapable of loving, Lavinia is incapable of being loved. Celia, however, gives a spiritual dimension to the play.

The play begins with a cocktail party being held in the house of Mr. Edward Chamberlayne, a barrister. The guests are Celia Copplestone, Alexander MacColgie Gibbs, Peter Quilp, Julia Shuttlewaite and a person who remained unidentified. What makes the situation highly embarrassing for the host is the mysterious disappearance of his wife, Lavinia. Edward, however, tries to keep up appearances and pretends that his wife has gone to pay a visit to an aunt in the country. So the guests leave, but an eccentric Unidentified Guest stays behind, who shows both an uncanny penetration into the host's state of mind and an apparent knowledge of his secret. Actually, it is Edward who had persuaded him to stay on and finish the cocktail:

"Don't go yet.
I very much want to talk to somebody;

And it's easier to talk to a person you don't know.
The fact is, that Lavinia has left me."[3]

During their conversation a great deal is revealed about the disharmony that underlined the relations between Edward and Lavinia. However, Edward says that he would like to have his wife back. But his desire to have Lavinia back is not the result of love, but rather a creation of his wounded pride and a desire to save his face in society. The Unidentified Guest simply advises him to 'Wait' and promises to bring her back, within the next twenty-four hours, but only on one condition:

"But if I bring her back it must be on one condition:
That you promise to ask her no questions
Of where she has been."[4]

Their conversation was once interrupted by Julia coming to collect her umbrella which she had forgotten and again when she comes with Peter looking for her glasses, which she later finds in her own bag. The Unidentified Guest leaves singing a drinking song. Naturally, Julia thinks him to be a "dreadful man."[5] Julia soon goes away but Peter stays behind because he wanted to consult Edward about some important matter. Peter was in a confiding mood and requests Edward to help him win Celia.

"The point is, I thought we had a great deal in common
And I think she thought so too."[6]

But now "she has simply faded—into some other picture—Like a film effect."[7] So, now he wants to find out what the reality is:

"I was saying, what is the reality
Of experience between two unreal people?"[8]

Edward promises to talk to Celia about this affair, while at heart he himself has feelings of love for her. Then, Alex also comes inviting him to have dinner with him. But Edward declines the invitation saying, "I rather *want* to be alone, this evening."[9] Alex then offers to cook his dinner and goes into his kitchen. But he keeps on popping while Edward and Peter are talking about Celia. Finally both Peter and Alex leave and after their departure Edward tries to talk to Celia on the phone, but doesn't get her. Here the scene closes.

The second scene of Act I is one of the most important and dramatically effective scenes of the play. It lays bare further emotional complications. Celia comes to the house of Edward urged by an irresistible desire to see him alone. It is apparent that Celia and Edward are carrying on an affair. But then it comes as a shock to Celia that Edward wants Lavinia back. Celia is afraid that Edward is just surrendering himself to panic and fatigue and advises him to see "a very great doctor whom I have heard of—and his name is Reilly,"[10] to which Edward replies:

"It would need someone greater than the greatest doctor
To cure *this* illness."[11]

Edward assures her that he considers her to be a very rare person, but finds that now it is too late. He realizes that he has not been fair to her and is sorry for it. At this Celia is greatly shocked to realize that her dream was over, and says that perhaps he took her only as "a passing diversion."[12] Edward felt hurt and so he also accuses Celia of flirting with Peter whom perhaps she used "as a passing diversion."[13] Celia then explains that Peter meant nothing to her. She only felt that he was lonely and friendless and so gave him company. There was nothing more between them. She also felt humiliated that she was indulging in an unreal dream and that Edward loved Lavinia and not her. At this stage Edward's emotions are also difficult to understand. He is not sure why he wants Lavinia back. He is rather shaken by his realization that he does not love Celia enough to begin his life afresh with her. Celia, however, doubts if Edward can at all be happy with Lavinia. But Edward feels that to be happy or unhappy does not depend upon the individual. As a matter of fact the fate of man is predetermined. The desire to escape one's fate is a mere delusion. He says:

"The self that can say 'I want this—or want that'—
The self that wills—he is a feeble creature;
He has to come to terms in the end
With the obstinate, the tougher self; who does not speak,
Who never talks, who cannot argue;
And who in some men may be the *guardian*"[14]

While Edward talks thus, a bitter revelation comes to Celia, which is a turning point in the life of Celia for she now grasps the reality that her relation with Edward was only an imperfect projection of something that her soul craved for:

"The man I saw before, he was only a projection—
I see that now—of something that I wanted
No, not *wanted*—something I aspired to—
Something I desperately wanted to exist."[15]

This state of mind of Celia prepares us for the choice that she makes in the consulting room of the psychiatrist. The two are thus reconciled and the scene ends with their drinking to the Guardians. Certainly Celia has grown and gained in spiritual stature in the course of this scene.

Then the third scene of Act I takes place in the same room of the Chamberlaynes. It is the afternoon of the next day. Edward is alone when the Unidentified Guest of the previous day's Cocktail Party drops into warn Edward once more of the seriousness of the decision he had taken in wanting to have Lavinia back and warns Edward that he is no longer free to change his mind:

"Your moment of freedom was yesterday
You made a decision. You set in motion
Forces in your life and in the lives of others
Which cannot be reversed."[16]

He has come there to tell him that his wife would come and it is a serious matter because it is not easy to bring some one "back from the dead"[17] indicating that the wife whom he knew is 'dead' and the one whom he would meet now would be an entirely different person. She would return soon and they must not waste their time in talking of the past or in asking/offering explanations, saying: "Don't strangle each other with knotted memories."[18]

As soon as the mysterious figure leaves and Edward is alone contemplating the prospect of the imminent meeting with his wife, some visitors arrive. They are Celia, Peter, Alex and Julia. All of them tell that they have come in response to telegrams received from Lavinia. Edward cannot understand anything. To him it is all so very confusing and perplexing. During the conversation that ensues Peter makes the announcement that he is going to California where he has got a contract for making films. This is followed by Celia's declaration that she is going away too (but doesn't know where). It is at this point that Lavinia enters greeting Celia and Peter with obvious surprise, for she has not the faintest idea of ever having sent telegrams to anyone. It is really a ludicrous situation. So after greetings are over the guests leave, so that the Chamberlaynes may be alone together and Lavinia, who looks so tired and exhausted, may have some rest.

Left alone, the two, husband and wife discover that both of them have much changed during the twenty-four hours. But as they start talking about their past they again relapse into the same old vicious circle of flinging accusations against each other. They find themselves back in the trap, and Edward realizes with anguish that he has no escape.

"There was a door
And I could not open it; I could not touch the handle
Why could I not walk out of my prison?"[19]

Lavinia feels that Edward is on the edge of a nervous breakdown and suggests that he should go to a doctor and says that she knows one who would be able to help him. Edward replies that if he at all sees a doctor, it would be one of his own choice and not one who has been tutored by her and who is likely to see things from her "point of view."[20] And the first Act concludes with Edward's despairing cry:

"O God, O God, if I could return to yesterday
Before I thought that I had made a decision."[21]

The next Act is set several weeks later in the consulting room of Sir Henry Harcourt Reilly, the Unidentified Guest of Act I, who turns out to be, not a brilliant madman, but a Harley Street psychiatrist. The situation that develops is the most dramatic in the whole play. As the curtain rises we see the doctor instructing his nurse-secretary to show three different patients, whom he is expecting, into three different rooms so that they do not see each other. It soon becomes clear that the disappearance of Lavinia was the result of a conspiracy between Julia, Alex and Sir Reilly. They have now arranged that both Edward and

Lavinia should come to consult the doctor separately. Later Celia is also to come to consult the doctor. Here we find Alex, Julia and Sir Henry playing the sober role of the 'Guardians.'

Edward is the first to arrive just to find to his great shock that Sir Henry Harcourt Reilly is none other than the Unidentified Guest of the cocktail party, who restored Lavinia to him. So his first impulse was to go away for he feels that a trap has been laid for him. But Sir Henry says soothingly:

"Let's not call it a trap
But if it is a trap, then you cannot escape from it."[22]

As such, Edward realizes that it is better to discuss his complaints. He tells the doctor that he is suffering from nervous breakdown, and is constantly haunted by a sense of his own insignificance. He wanted his wife to return because without her he felt helpless, oppressed with a sense of unreality. He wants himself to be put into some sanatorium where he might be alone. If this were not possible he would like to move to some hotel. But Reilly knows only too well that Edward, in describing his symptoms, is hiding a lot and he takes the unusual step of introducing an indignant Edward to another patient, none other than Lavinia. The protest expressed by Edward is also shared by Lavinia too who says as soon as she enters the room:

"Well, Sir Henry!
I said I would come to talk about my husband
I didn't say I was prepared to meet him."[23]

The doctor, then, tactfully makes them discuss their problems and difficulties in his presence. It transpires that they have much in common. They both have been in love, the one with Celia and the other with Peter. They both have tried to conceal their love affairs from the doctor whom they came to consult. In both cases the love has come to nothing. They are both alike in their nature and temperament, as Reilly says:

"And now you begin to see, I hope,
How much you have in common. The same isolation
A man who finds himself incapable of loving
And a woman who finds that no man can love her."[24]

They had been accusing each other of their own faults, and so they could not understand each other. So if instead of finding faults with each other they tried to understand their own shortcomings, they might reach a sort of working arrangement and life together may yet be possible for them. They must therefore go back to their own home and try to make "the best of a bad job."[25] The parting words of the doctor to them are "Go in peace, And work out your salvation with diligence."[26]

When the Chamberlaynes are gone, Julia enters to tell Sir Henry that the third patient is ready, though slightly reluctant. When Julia withdraws to the next room, Celia Copplestone enters and recognizes Sir Henry. But without wasting his time Celia tries to describe her condition, which has brought her to him. She says, "I at least have no one to blame but myself."[27] Her peculiar trouble is an awareness of solitude; but it is a peculiar sense of loneliness:

"...it isn't that I *want* to be alone,
But that everyone's alone—or so it seems to me,
They make noises, and they think they are talking to each other;
They make faces; and think they understand each other.
And I'm sure they don't. Is that a delusion."[28]

With this sense of loneliness Celia also feels something strange, which she tentatively describes as a sense of sin. But this sense of sin in not caused by her having been immoral or her having hurt others.

"It's not the feeling of anything I've *ever done*
Which I might get away from, or of anything in me
I could get rid of—but of emptiness, of failure
Towards someone, or something outside of myself
And I feel I must...*atone*—is that the word?
Can you treat a patient for such a state of mind?"[29]

Thus Celia was left with an aching sense of loneliness. Desperately she asks Reilly if he can cure her. Reilly points out that the condition is curable but that the form of treatment is to be her own *choice*. He says, she could reconcile herself to the human condition and catching some sort of happiness from a life of common routine where the important thing is to:

"Learn to avoid excessive expectation,
Become tolerant, of themselves and others."[30]

This way of life has its justification and is not devoid of glory. "In a world of lunacy, violence, stupidity and greed...it is a good life."[31] But he also points out that there is another way for the courageous, and for those who have faith—'the kind of faith that issues from despair.' However, the end of the way or the destination cannot be described and the journey is blind. Celia chooses the second alternative and with the trust of a child she places herself entirely in his hands. So, finally with the spiritual strength and compassion of a father confessor, Reilly advises Celia:

"Go in peace, my daughter
Work out your salvation with diligence."[32]

When Celia is gone Julia comes in and it is now that we know something about the path along which Reilly has directed Celia—the path that leads to sainthood. Though confident that Celia will go far, both Sir Henry and Julia seem to be afraid about her future:

"...What do we know of the terrors of the journey?
You and I don't know the process by which the human is Transhumanised."[33]

With Alex, the third of the Guardians joining them they utter a ritualistic chant invoking the blessings of the protector of travelers:

"Protect her from the Voices
Protect her from the Visions
Protect her in the tumult
Protect her in the silence."[34]

Then talking about Peter Quilpe, Reilly says, "He has not yet come to where the words are valid."[35] And the second Act closes.

In Act III we are taken once again to the drawing room of the Chamberlaynes' London flat. The time is two years later. Lavinia is getting ready for another cocktail party. Edward arrives early and from the affectionate teasing he gives her it is evident that the prayer spoken by the Guardians for the building of the hearth has borne fruit. Their concern for each other's well-being is refreshing. The guests—Julia, Alex, Reilly and Peter arrive one after the other. Initially their conversation is about frivolous topics, but as it takes a serious turn Peter informs that he is making a film on English life in California and asks if someone can tell him where Celia Copplestone is, so that he could ask her to join him in the films. But Alex, who has come straight from Kinkanja, puts an end to his hopes by imparting the unexpected news of Celia's death. To the shocked group, Alex explains how Celia was crucified very near an anthill during an insurrection of the natives of Kinkanja. Celia was working there as a Christian missionary nurse, looking after the plague stricken natives. Reilly says that her end was the result of her own 'choice' and so no one was to be blamed for it. It was her destiny to die in this way. As Julia says:

"Everyone makes a choice, of one kind or another
And then must take the consequences."[36]

And further adds:

"And now the consequence of the Chamberlaynes' choice
Is a cocktail party."[37]

Edward, however, learns that "every moment is a fresh beginning; and that life is only keeping on,"[38] and somehow the two ideas seem to fit together. The Guardians and Peter quietly slip off leaving the Chamberlaynes to hold their party. Finally the doorbell rings announcing the arrival of the guest and the play comes to a close as the cocktail party gets going. "Anyhow, we are reminded of the first and last lines of *East Coker*: *In my beginning is my end./ In my end is my beginning.*"[39]

Thus, we find that "the play is essentially about human condition within the framework of marriage and outside it. Each person in his relationship with others has been crusted over with illusion about himself and others with the result that he has developed a personality, which is largely false and artificial. Somewhere beneath this facade lies his true self. Before he can achieve a meaningful and satisfactory life, he must somehow strip away the illusion and recognize the deeper, tougher self."[40]

"He has come to terms in the end
With the obstinate tougher self; who does not speak,
Who never talks, who cannot argue;
And who in some men may be the *Guardian*."[41]

The Chamberlaynes have been married for five years but their life has been dull, unhappy and wretched. There is lack of understanding and sympathy, there is moral turpitude and as a result the family is bound to disintegrate. The play depicts two ways of life, chosen by characters who are differently endowed with spiritual qualities. It is thus concerned with discipline in the life of the common man, as well as in the life of the saints. Hence the question of choice assumes great significance in the play. The story of Edward and Celia is a revealing commentary on the most talked about and the least exercised of human privileges, that is, the right of free choice in our lives.

The play deals with different levels of spiritual experience—of the saints and of the mortals. Each is offered a choice and the choice determines their future lives. As Julia says:

"Everyone makes a choice, of one kind or another
And then must take the consequences."[42]

Celia's choice, although she doesn't realize it at that time, constitutes a life of potential sainthood. The psychiatrist shows her two distinct paths. "Carol Smith interprets the two ways of life mentioned by Sir Henry as the Christian mystic's twofold ways of reaching God: the Negative Way by which the soul comes to be united with God by divesting itself of the love of created Beings, and the Affirmative Way by which it accepts all creatures as images of the Divine."[43] "Thus the characters move on two planes: the surface reality and the underlying emotional reality implicating a ritual."[44] But as Reilly himself says:

"Neither way is better,
Both ways are necessary, It is also necessary
To make a choice between them."[45]

Reilly the psychiatrist-cum-spiritual advisor sends Celia along the torturous path because he realizes that she has something that others do not have. In her passionate desire for atonement she readily embraces the goal pointed out to her by Sir Henry.

Celia becomes ready for this great goal by the sacrifice of her own will, which in a way is her first martyrdom. "Celia's choice, though she does not perceive it, constitutes a life of potential sainthood."[46] However, the path she has chosen is beset with difficulties. Julia tells Sir Henry about Celia:

> "O, yes she will go far. And we know where she is going
> But what do we know of the terrors of the journey?
> You and I don't know the process by which the human is Transhumanised."[47]

And again in answer to Henry's question, "Will she be frightened by the first appearance of projected spirits?" Julia replies:

> "Henry you simply do not understand innocence
> She will be afraid of nothing; She will not even know
> That there is anything there to be afraid of
> She is too humble. She will pass between the scolding hills,
> Through the valley of derision, like a child sent on an errand
> In eagerness and patience. Yet she must suffer."[48]

Armed with this innocence and this humility Celia goes towards her death, martyrdom in fact. As Grover Smith says, "She is ready for dedication by the sacrifice of her own will—her first martyrdom. Her second martyrdom, her sacrifice by death, simply ratifies her patient humility."[49] She dies a cruel and painful death, for she is crucified on an anthill in Kinkanja during an insurrection of the natives. Celia's death is highly symbolic. All the martyrs in Eliot's plays have something Christ-like about them. Her second martyrdom is her death. Celia's martyrdom has a tremendous influence on the lives of others. But the theme of the play is more than martyrdom. "In her martyrdom she suffers physical death but achieves eternal life, just as she achieves another kind of Christian marriage in the union of the saint with God."[50]

Nevertheless, Edward's choice of reconciliation in domestic life and Celia's choice of martyrdom are invariably regulated by Sir Henry's spiritual guidance. "The emphasis on choice for both the Chamberlaynes and Celia is another manifestation of the idea of Christian freedom. Choice is free for the Christian, but the price of the wrong choice is a stage of death-in-life, while the reward of the right choice is the ultimate illumination."[51]

As we have seen in all the plays of Eliot there is always an under pattern of myth in his plays. "He thinks that myths are the common inheritance of the dramatist and the audience which can bind them together and provide a *Universe of discourse.*"[52] Although as far as *The Cocktail Party* is concerned it was only when Eliot pointed out that his play was based on Alcestis by Euripides that critics began to notice the similarity between these two plays.

Alcestis by Euripides dramatizes the story of Admetus, the King of Pherae and how he is saved from death by the willing sacrifice of his wife Alcestis, who dies in his place. The play shows how Alcestis is restored from death to her husband by the great Heracles.

When the play begins, we find how Admetus is weighed down by the grief that has visited his house. We learn how the gods promised that Admetus would escape from death if someone would consent to die in his place. Even his aged parents refused to do so but Alcestis, his wife voluntarily offered to die for him. Into the household oppressed by sorrow Heracles the son of Jove comes seeking hospitality, on his way to a difficult mission. Rather than reveal to this illustrious guest the cause of his mourning, Admetus chooses to keep the guest in the dark as to the nature of catastrophe that has come to him.

Heracles thus, with no idea of the sorrow that afflicts Alcestis and his household goes on drinking and making merry. Even the servants feel that his jocular conduct ill accords with the calamity that has befallen the house. Gradually Heracles learns the terrible truth and is filled with self-reproach.

Then self-reproach and regret yield to a firm resolve to restore the lady to Admetus. He swears to wrestle with the "sable-vested tyrant of the death" for the sake of Alcestis and if he cannot win her that way, to go to Pluto and his Queen and "beg her thence."

With this resolution Heracles leaves the house of Admetus and when he returns, it is with Alcestis. But she is veiled and when Heracles urges Admetus to take her in, Admetus refuses to accept her, for in his heart he still cherishes the memory of the wife whom he has entombed. But later when he recognizes his well-beloved wife, he is overwhelmed with joy. His heart welling up with thankfulness, he tells Heracles: "O, be thou blest, thou generous son of Jove!"

Explaining his debt to Euripides, Eliot cited as an example the conduct of the Unidentified Guest in the house of the Chamberlaynes. Reilly, in fact, resembles Heracles in many respects. Each arrives at a house where there has been a loss, the loss of the wife. Hence Reilly has come as much to a house of death as Heracles in Alcestis. The conduct of these two people in the house of death also evinces much similarity. Thus by the use of the myth Eliot creates a double pattern in the play. The audience discerns one meaning at the surface level while the myth invokes another meaning at the deeper level. In this way with all its symbolism and suggestivity the mythical method works as a latent chorus.

We find that in *The Cocktail Party* Celia, Edward, Lavinia and Peter are *Seekers*. Celia and the Chamberlaynes see the light, though in different ways, much before Peter does, and in the last scene, the Chamberlaynes actually try to teach Peter what they have themselves learnt. Reilly, the chief *Helper* is ably assisted by Julia and Alex, the *Guardians*. It is Reilly who brings Lavinia back. Again it is he, who tells Edward how futile it has been on his part to have concealed from Lavinia his secret relation with Celia. He also admonishes Lavinia for her attachment to Peter. Thus he pinpoints the basic similarity in their nature and temperament:

"And now you begin to see, I hope
How much you have in common. The same isolation
A man finds himself incapable of loving
And a woman who finds that no man can love her."[53]

Finally, he gives the benediction, which has the force of "Go in peace. And work out your salvation with diligence."[54] Thus, as Parwati Singh says, "Eliot has put in the mouth of Reilly the very parting message which Buddha had given to his disciples."[55]

He advises Edward not to "strangle each other with knotted memories."[56]

In this way, Eliot in *The Cocktail Party* tries to invigorate the life of the spirit and strengthen the bonds of society. "Before the party itself begins, a crucifixion has been recalled and a vicarious atonement recognized. The cocktail party, can be the secular counterpart of the Communion Service if given in the right spirit, the titbits and the short drinks are the equivalents of the bread and wine. The play is almost a piece of Metaphysical wit in its discovery of analogy in unlikely places."[57]

Although after *The Family Reunion*, Eliot drops the formal use of the chorus in his subsequent plays, yet in some form or the other the choric function continues to be performed by the use of certain special devices and symbols. "The truth is that while *The Cocktail Party* contains no chorus, no Eumenides, and no lyrical duets, the anti realistic forces which it utilizes are deployed with much greater success than in *The Family Reunion.*"[58] As D.E. Jones says, "In his capacity as the psychiatrist, Reilly is the fashionable modern substitute for the priest, and the psychiatrist's couch is the substitute for the confessional box. But he is a poor substitute, unable to understand the advice he gives; he ask Julia about Celia's experiences on the journey in which 'the human is Transhumanised"[59] and admits that:

"When I say to one like her
'Work out your salvation with diligence', I do not understand
What I myself am saying."[60]

The Cocktail Party creates quite a new and convincing symbols in the 'Guardians.' D.E. Jones correctly remarks that their alienation from the common people is possibly a dramatic device to heighten the tone of the play. "Guardianship is, so to speak, the machinery of the plot. As instruments of a higher power, the Guardians contrive a good deal of the action of the play. In this way symbolism becomes highly functional and contrariwise their manipulation of the plot assumes a metaphysical significance and suggests the way Divine Providence works in society."[61]

"In the absence of these Guardians the plot of *The Cocktail Party* would suffer a total wreck, as the activities of other characters are, more or less, regulated by their clever manoeuvres. Reilly, the chief Guardian is responsible for all the major decision taken by the Chamberlaynes as well as Celia."[62] To borrow the words of V.K. Roy, "Sir Henry functions, in this play, is as a catalytic agent with the help of Julia and Alex."[63] In this way, "Sir Henry Harcourt Reilly has many functions to perform. He acts as an Unidentified guest, an experienced psychiatrist, divine investigator and spiritual surgeon."[64] But the most significant role of Sir Henry is like that of Agatha, who "acts as an auxiliary chorus, because the function of the main chorus is to represent obtuse humanity, someone is necessary to interpret the action more perceptibly."[65] In this respect the Guardians have become the mouthpiece of Eliot's philosophy and continue to perform the Choric function with subtlety.

It must be said to the credit of Eliot that instead of leaving the 'Guardians' as a mere philosophical concept, he has made them vitally important and has given to them a highly dramatic role. In this respect the Guardians of *The Cocktail Party* are an infinitely more successful and satisfactory dramatic device than the Eumenides of *The Family Reunion*.

"The important thing about the Guardians here is that they initiate Celia and the Chamberlaynes into vocations according to their potentialities. Celia is capable of full enlightenment; Edward and Lavinia, less gifted, remain partly blind, in the dark. The figuratively 'one-eyed' Sir Henry and the broken-spectacled, sibyllic Julia are interpreters of light to darkness."[66]

"Thus, by the divinely operated circle of reciprocal cures wrought by Eliot's three guardians, what begins as a comedy of misdirected love affairs and marriage triangles, is transformed into an exposition of the multiple meanings of Christian love and marriage."[67]

In *The Cocktail Party* Eliot has "sacrificed almost all the obvious poetic devices and renounced his attempt to revive the conventions of the earlier poetic drama, apart from the basic convention of the verse itself. There are no quasi-soliloquies, no lyrical duets. The element of ritual and choric speaking are reduced to a very short section, the libation at the end of Act II and this is rather like a solemn form of toast to the absent friends."[68]

"And now we are ready to proceed to the libation.
Alex   : The words for the building of the hearth.
[*They raise their glasses*]
Reilly : Let them build the hearth
         Under the protection of the stars.
Alex   : Let them place a chair each side of it.
Julia : May the holy ones watch over the roof.
         May the moon herself influence the bed.
[*They drink*]
Alex   : The words for those who go upon a journey.
Reilly : Protector of travellers
         Bless the road.
Allex : Watch over her in the desert
         Watch over her in the mountain
         Watch over her in the labyrinth.
         Watch over her by the quicksand.
Julia : Protect her from the Voices.
         Protect her from the Visions
         Protect her in the tumult
         Protect her in the silences.
[*They drink*]"[69]

"Sir Henry's ritual identity is suggested by his continuous drinking of gin with drops of water (he is adulterating his spiritual nature with a drop of water, representing time, flux and humanity). His buffoonery and bawdy revelry are echoes of the traditional actions of the cook-doctor who hides his curative power and canny ability to outwit his opponents in the guise of a fool."[70]

According to Dennis Donough, "Eliot appears to have planned that this character would overflow every vessel, however large, however whole. He never allows us to forget the symbolic function of Reilly, Julia and Alex as *Guardians*: We have continual impression of mysterious forces in action and Psychiatry takes on a spiritual dimension."[71] The minor characters, who at first seemed so tiresome—the interfering old woman (Julia) and the helpful man of the world (Alex) turn out to be in benevolent league with the doctor who effects the cures and all work together for good.

"*The Cocktail Party* presents an even more difficult problem. We must consider it (however hesitantly) as a tragedy; because of its ritual element, its atonement for guilt, the sacrificial death of Celia, and its religious framework."[72]

"Though the verse used in *The Cocktail Party* cautiously guards itself against any superfluity of poetic elevation and almost vies with prose in its strict adherence to everyday speech rhythm, it is able to reflect the vitality of poetic imagination.... Eliot has successfully experimented with a kind of verse that can easily pass from the commonplace and prosaic tone of conversation in a drawing-room to a serious, reflective, and impassioned speech, without ever giving the audience any opportunity to be conscious of the medium."[73]

Raymond Williams speaks of Eliot's successful experiment in verse medium in *The Cocktail Party* in glowing terms. He describes it as a "development of a flexible, lucid verse manner, based very closely on speech and yet capable of greatest precision and distinction, is unquestionably a major achievement."[74]

So in our final analysis, we can say that *The Cocktail Party* is a great step forward in Eliot's endeavours to revive the drama. In this play he integrates tragedy with comedy. He interfuses speech and poetry in such a manner that poetry while retaining its essential character, sounds like speech. He combines Pagan myth with Christian values and presents it before a 20th century audience. Finally even while discarding the formal use of the chorus, he interfuses the chorus into the characters of the play by devising the special machinery of the *Guardians*, who besides being the mouthpiece of the dramatist also guide the action of the play and make a meaningful commentary on other characters and thus perform important choric functions. Thus the chorus has been introduced into the play with a mask and yet has a powerful identity as its 'dramatic personae,' the reason being Eliot's gradual but positive shift from the Theatre of Ideas to the Theatre of Character.

Hence it will have to be minutely studied how Eliot in his later plays where he abandons the formal use of the chorus, adopts compensatory devices which will fill the vacuum so caused, because the choric function continues to be performed by some device or the other.

NOTES AND REFERENCES

1. Smith, Grover. 2000. *T.S. Eliot's Poetry and Plays—A Study in Sources and Meaning*. Chicago: The University of Chicago Press, First Indian Reprint. New Delhi: Doaba Publications. 222.
2. Smith, Carol H. 1963. *T.S. Eliot's Dramatic Theory and Practice*. London: Oxford University Press. 166.
3. Eliot, T.S. 1969. *The Complete Poems and Plays of T.S. Eliot*. London: Faber and Faber. 359-60.
4. *Ibid.* 364.
5. *Ibid.* 365.
6. *Ibid.* 367.
7. *Ibid.* 370.
8. *Ibid.* 371.
9. *Ibid.* 368.
10. *Ibid.* 378-79.
11. *Ibid.* 379.
12. *Ibid.* 380.
13. *Ibid.*
14. *Ibid.* 381.
15. *Ibid.* 382.
16. Ibid. 384.
17. *Ibid.*
18. *Ibid.* 385.
19. *Ibid.* 397.
20. *Ibid.*
21. *Ibid.* 398.
22. *Ibid.* 401.
23. *Ibid.* 405.

24. *Ibid.* 410.
25. *Ibid.*
26. *Ibid.* 411.
27. *Ibid.* 413.
28. *Ibid.* 414.
29. *Ibid.* 416.
30. *Ibid.* 417.
31. *Ibid.* 418.
32. *Ibid.* 420.
33. *Ibid.* 421.
34. *Ibid.* 422.
35. *Ibid.*
36. *Ibid.* 439.
37. *Ibid.*
38. *Ibid.* 440.
39. Titus, T.K. 2001. *A Critical Study of T.S. Eliot's Works*. New Delhi: Atlantic Publishers & Distributors (P) Ltd. 107.
40. Singh, Parwati. 1988. *Character and Symbol in the Plays of T.S. Eliot*. Delhi: Capital Publishing House. 98.
41. Eliot, T.S. 1969. *The Complete Poems and Plays of T.S. Eliot*. London: Faber and Faber. 381.
42. *Ibid.* 439.
43. Sarkar, Subhas. 2006. *T.S. Eliot—The Dramatist*. New Delhi: Atlantic Publishers & Distributors (P) Ltd. 189.
44. *Ibid.* 193.
45. Eliot, T.S. 1969. *The Complete Poems and Plays of T.S. Eliot*. London: Faber and Faber. 418.
46. Smith, Grover. 2000. *T.S. Eliot's Poetry and Plays—A Study in Sources and Meaning*. Chicago: The University of Chicago Press, First Indian Reprint. New Delhi: Doaba Publications. 215.
47. Eliot, T.S. 1969. *The Complete Poems and Plays of T.S. Eliot*. London: Faber and Faber. 421.
48. *Ibid.*
49. Smith, Grover. 2000. *T.S. Eliot's Poetry and Plays—A Study in Sources and Meaning*. Chicago: The University of Chicago Press, First Indian Reprint. New Delhi: Doaba Publications. 225.
50. Smith, Carol H. 1963. *T.S. Eliot's Dramatic Theory and Practice*. London: Oxford University Press. 178-79.

51. *Ibid.* 179.
52. Sarkar, Subhas. 2006. *T.S. Eliot—The Dramatist.* New Delhi: Atlantic Publishers & Distributors (P) Ltd. 202.
53. Eliot, T.S. 1969. *The Complete Poems and Plays of T.S. Eliot.* London: Faber and Faber. 410.
54. *Ibid.* 411.
55. Singh, Dr. Parwati. 1988. *Character and Symbol in the Plays of T.S. Eliot.* Delhi: Capital Publishing House. 92.
56. Eliot, T.S. 1969. *The Complete Poems and Plays of T.S. Eliot.* London: Faber and Faber. 385.
57. Jones, D.E. 1960. *The Plays of T.S. Eliot.* London: Routledge & Kegan Paul. 143.
58. Kenner, Hugh. 1962. *Twentieth Century Views: T.S. Eliot.* New Jersey: Prentice Hall. 175.
59. Jones, D.E. 1960. *The Plays of T.S. Eliot.* London: Routledge & Kegan Paul. 152.
60. Eliot, T.S. 1969. *The Complete Poems and Plays of T.S. Eliot.* London: Faber and Faber. 421.
61. Jones, D.E. 1960. *The Plays of T.S. Eliot.* London: Routledge & Kegan Paul. 152-53.
62. Sarkar, Subhas. 2006. *T.S. Eliot—The Dramatist.* New Delhi: Atlantic Publishers & Distributors (P) Ltd. 183.
63. Roy, V.K. 1979. *T.S. Eliot—Quest for Belief.* Delhi: Ajanta Publications. 331.
64. Sharma, H.L. 1976. *T.S. Eliot—His Dramatic Theories.* New Delhi: S. Chand & Co. 147.
65. Jones, D.E. 1960. *The Plays of T.S. Eliot.* London: Routledge & Kegan Paul. 104.
66. Smith, Grover. 2000. *T.S. Eliot's Poetry and Plays—A Study in Sources and Meaning.* Chicago: The University of Chicago Press, First Indian Reprint. New Delhi: Doaba Publications. 220.
67. Smith, Carol H. 1963. *T.S. Eliot's Dramatic Theory and Practice.* London: Oxford University Press. 154.
68. Jones, D.E. 1960. *The Plays of T.S. Eliot.* London: Routledge & Kegan Paul. 124.
69. Eliot, T.S. 1969. *The Complete Poems and Plays of T.S. Eliot.* London: Faber and Faber. 422.
70. Smith, Carol H. 1963. *T.S. Eliot's Dramatic Theory and Practice.* London: Oxford University Press. 179.

71. Kenner, Hugh. 1962. *Twentieth Century Views*: *T.S. Eliot*. New Jersey: Prentice Hall. 179.
72. Henn, T.R. 1956. *The Harvest of Tragedy*. London: Methuen & Co. Ltd. 225-26.
73. Sarkar, Subhas. 2006. *T.S. Eliot—The Dramatist*. New Delhi: Atlantic Publishers & Distributors (P) Ltd. 177-78.
74. *Ibid*. 180.

6 *The Elder Statesman*

The Elder Statesman, first performed at Edinburgh festival in 1958, directs our attention to an elder statesman in his retired life. He has been honoured and applauded in his role as a statesman. But now on his deathbed, he sees for the first time the reflections of his true self, of a life spent in avoiding reality and the sense of guilt, which comes from moral cowardice. The play is simpler in conception and human in treatment.

The play opens in the drawing room of Lord Claverton, in London with a love scene between Monica and her suitor Charles. "The developing relationship between the young lovers is used throughout the play to exert an emotional control over the other events and to reflect the effect of these events upon their love.... Their conversation states the theme which is developed throughout the stages of Lord Claverton's spiritual re-education."[1]

As the curtain rises we find Charles and Monica engaged in conversation expressing their love for each other, but Monica is hesitating to marry Charles immediately because it will make her father feel more lonely and also because Lord Claverton fears being exposed to strangers. So far people had seen him in his garb of authority but now being shorn of all his former plumes he is scared of the vacuum he feels in his own life. Although Monica asks him to take life easily, but he cannot do it. He says:

"To take life easily. Take life easily!
It's like telling a man he mustn't run for trains
When the last thing he wants is to take a train for any where!"[2]

Just then Frederico Gomez, who was Fred Culverwell before, appears on the scene. Gomez and Claverton were friends in their younger days at Oxford. They recall having committed an act of criminality in their younger days. They took two girls for enjoyment, drove fast and killed an old man by running over him. Claverton had developed expensive tastes in his friend who was also once jailed for certain illegal acts. Gomez then left England and settled in San Marco a Central American Republic where he amassed a great amount of wealth by illegal business. He also changed his name and has now returned to England after 30 years when he felt homesick and lonely. He says:

"O God, Dick, *you* don't know what it is like
To be so cut off! Homesickness!"[3]

But when Claverton also says he feels lonely, Gomez replies:

"Oh, loneliness—
Everybody knows what that's like.
Your loneliness—so cosy, warm and padded:
You are not isolated—merely insulated."[4]

Gomez and Claverton are both 60 now. While they talk to each other the past haunt them. But they are now tired of their lives and want to make friends of each other again. But Lord Claverton fights shy of his past and wants to terminate his meeting with Gomez. But Gomez while trying to expose the mask of Lord Claverton says that both of them have been failures, but according to him Claverton is a greater failure because:

"The worst kind of failure, in my opinion,
Is the man who has to keep on pretending to himself
That he's a success—the man who in the morning
Has to make up his face before he looks in the mirror."[5]

His moral cowardice is also brought forth in his ludicrous attempt at shirking to accept the moral responsibility for the downfall of Gomez. But Gomez promises him that he has not come to blackmail him on any account. On the contrary Gomez offers to revive his friendship with him just to help him if he needs his help:

"You were generous friend to me once
As you pointedly reminded me a moment ago.
Now it's my turn, perhaps, to do you a kindness."[6]

And as Gomez departs Monica tell him that he needs rest because this interview has worn him out.

Then Act II opens at the terrace of Badgley Court, a health resort, where the doctors of Claverton have sent him for rest and recovery. "Medical imagery and the presence of a doctor figure, which have recurred in virtually all of Eliot's plays, are present in a more overt form in *The Elder Statesman*. Lord Claverton is ill, both literally and figuratively."[7] Monica is with him for company. Busybody Mrs. Piggott briefs them about the various amenities of the nursing home and then Mrs. Carghill appears on the scene, who had once fallen in love with Claverton. She was a stage actress, beautiful and sprightly and at that time her name was Maisie Montjoy. When she talks of her love to Lord Claverton, he feels very uncomfortable and asks her to bury the old memories, on which she psychologises:

"A man may prefer to forget all the women
He has love. But a woman doesn't want to forget
A single one of her admirers. Why even a faithless lover
Is still, in her memory, a kind of testimonial
Men live by forgetting—women live on memories."[8]

Mrs. Carghil also tells Lord Claverton that she could have ruined his career, if she wanted; and so in this respect she at least negatively laid the foundation of Claverton's life: "So perhaps I laid the foundation of your fortunes!"[9] In turn Lord Claverton tells her that he laid the foundation of her life of art, because Claverton's father somehow broke his son away from this engagement by offering a large sum of money to her. Mrs. Carghill though now not in love with him still reads each night the love letters, which Claverton once wrote her. She had shown some of these letters to a few of her friends and one of them (Effie) said: "If he becomes a famous man/ And you should be in want, you could have these letters auctioned."[10] But just then Mrs. Piggott enters and as Mrs. Carghill leaves she sympathetically makes a remark, which is full of irony:

"If she bothers you again
Just let me know. I'm afraid it's the penalty
Of being famous."[11]

Meanwhile, by an interesting interplay of the light and the serious this act provides the necessary complication in the action. But behind the screen of humour Eliot conceals the serious intentions of the play. Eliot actually wants to drive home the idea that Lord Claverton must work out his salvation by breaking through his self-created delusions to reach for the benediction of love. But prior to this illumination he must pass through the different stages of hell and purgatory.

However, the ultimate complication in action arises when Monica informs her father that Michael was in a hurry to see him. She is apprehensive that "something unpleasant has happened."[12] Lord Claverton meets his son Michael, who wants to lead a life of his own. The young man wants to go away to a foreign country to liberate himself from the influence of his father and fulfil his own ambitions through his own efforts.

"I was just your son—that is to say,
A kind of prolongation of your existence,
A representative carrying on business in your absence."[13]

The manner in which he wants to break away from his past life, Michael only mirrors his father's attitude. But Lords Claverton tries to persuade him saying:

"Believe me. Michael:
Those who flee from their past will always lose the race
I know this from experience."[14]

But his son rebels against him and challenges the propriety of his own code of moral conduct. But just at this juncture Monica arrives on the scene and exhorts them to love each other, underlining the importance of love and understanding within the family, which even transcends the formal communication through words:

"But there is no vocabulary
For love within a family, love that's lived in
But not looked at, love within the light of which
All else is seen, the love within which
All other love finds speech.
This love is silent."[15]

These lines echo the dedicatory poem in which Eliot speaks to his wife:

"The words mean what they say,
but some have a further meaning
For you and me only"[16]

Thus, Eliot seems to uphold the primacy of intuitive understanding above the verbal communication. Just at this stage Mrs. Carghill and Gomez enter and Lord Claverton finds himself haunted from all sides by the ghost of the past, from whom he wants to escape. He realizes that he cannot escape his past like a coward, but on the other hand confession, penitence and love can make him aware of his true self.

"What I want to escape from
Is myself, is the past. But what a coward I am.
To talk of escaping! And what a hypocrite!
A few minutes ago I was pleading with Michael
Not to try to escape from his own past failures:
I said I know from experience.
Do I understand the meaning?
Of the lesson I would teach."[17]

Just at this note of anguish and self-realization Act II ends.

Then, Act III again opens at the terrace of Badgley Court in the afternoon of the following day setting the stage for the confession of guilt by the hero. Love is once again brought to rescue the situation. Lord Claverton says to Charles:

"If a man has one person, just one in his life,
To whom he is willing to confer everything—
And that includes, mind you, not only things criminal,
Not only turpitude, meanness and cowardice,
But also situations, which are simply ridiculous
When he has played the fool (as who has not?)
Then he loves that person, and his love will save him!"[18]

Thereafter, through his confession of guilt to his daughter and to Charles, Lord Claverton makes a clean breast of his past failings. All the apprehensions of social blackmail are swept away by his recognition of reality and by his acceptance of the

The Elder Statesman

"ghosts" of his past as significant forces of his life. By confronting the spectres of the corrupted life of his past in Senor Gomez and Mrs. Carghill, he realizes the futility of escaping from his past sins.

"They are merely ghosts:
Spectres from my past. They've always been with me
Though it was not till lately that I found the living persons
Whose ghosts tormented me, to be only human beings,
Malicious, petty, and I see myself emerging
From my spectral existence into something like reality."[19]

Like Macbeth, Lord Claverton is being persecuted by the wrongs done by him. He is haunted by ghosts—the ghosts of his past deeds and misdeeds. But finally as he faces the reality he gathers courage to face his past boldly. He tells Monica and Charles:

"I shan't run away now—run away from *them*.
It is through this meeting that I shall at last escape them.
—I've made my confession to you, Monica:
That is the first step taken towards my freedom,
And perhaps the most important."[20]

He even appreciates these "ghosts" of his past for making him aware of the reality of things, of his true self, which he has always kept hidden under the mask of his deceptive self. He now feels the filial love he had not felt till now. He says:

"I've been freed from the self that pretends to be someone;
And in becoming no one, I begin to live."[21]

Eliot, however, deliberately keeps the story of Lord Claverton's moral struggle off the stage. Immediately after his final encounter with his "ghosts" who carry away Michael from him, the hero passes into a state of spiritual illumination and beatitude and the play ends in a ritual setting of Lord Claverton's death. But Eliot has deftly chosen to override the realistic convention to communicate to the audience the symbolic meaning of Lord Claverton's death—the serenity attained through martyrdom. "Like a sinner in a Morality play who comes to be absolved of his sin by confession, he makes a clean breast of the dark secrets of his life to his daughter and dies with the happiness of understanding of the all-engrossing power of love."[22] "He blesses the lovers as he leaves them, and the action of the play concludes, as it began, with a love scene between Monica and Charles in which they face together the knowledge and meaning of Lord Claverton's death."[23] In Lord Claverton's suffering and death they find rebirth as 'a new person who is you and me together.'[24] The play ends as Charles says, 'The dead has poured out a blessing on the living.'[25]

Thus, we find that the first act of the play offers an exposition of the elder statesman's loneliness and its relation to his shady past. Then Act II complicates the action by further exposing Lord Claverton's deceptive life. We find Claverton making frantic effort to save Michael from those mistakes, which he himself has committed. Finally in Act III, Eliot offers the resolution of these complications through Lord Claverton's acceptance of reality and his realization of the power of love.

According to Subhas Sarkar, "One can trace the source of this drama of self-deception in *The Love Song of J. Alfred Prufrock*, where two conflicting selves—the inner self and the public-self (or the external self) are at loggerhead. Prufrock is aware of the futility of escaping from one's true self."[26] The same story has been told in the livelier mould of drama in *The Elder Statesman*, where from a stage of vacuum and moral cowardice Lord Claverton reaches the positive stage of Goodness in life and feels that love in all its manifestations must be respected.

"But we should respect love always when we meet it;
Even when it's vain and selfish, we must not abuse it."[27]

Thus the central character of the play is Lord Claverton, an elderly ailing public figure who has been successful without ever rising as high as he once expected himself to be. He is pursued in his retirement by two ghosts from his early life. These are Mrs. Carghill (formerly Maisia Montjoy), who once sued him for breach of promise but settled out of court and Fred Culverwell (now known as Federico Gomez), whom he led into extravagant ways at Oxford and who later emigrated after serving a prison sentence for forgery. These people, now well off on their own account, are blackmailing him. They spend their time reminding him of his guilt, of how his public image does not match the real man underneath it. In the course of the play, he is led to face his own past for the first time, and to recognize and repudiate the element of "pretence" in his own public role. He confesses his youthful sins to his daughter and her fiancé:

"It is harder to confess the sin that one believes in
Than the crime that every one can appreciate."[28]

And as a result finds peace

"I feel at peace now.
It is the peace that ensues upon contrition."[29]

Or as Monica, his daughter puts it:

"In becoming no one, he has become himself."[30]

The Elder Statesman, thus, is the history of the hollowness of the life of Lord Claverton about whom Peter Milward says: "He is a man who is always playing a part in the eyes of the world, posing as someone he really is not, while all the time he is as it were locked out of his inner, private self; and in consequence, when he is left alone, he has nothing to contemplate within himself. Lord Claverton, thus, is a veritable pretender: he pretends not only with others but also with himself,"[31] as Gomez says:

"The man who has to keep on pretending to himself
That he's a success—the man who in the morning
Has to make up his face before he looks in the mirror."[32]

Lord Claverton is not a single man; rather he is modern humanity or life. Through him Eliot depicts the conditions of man in the modern society. Thus, "the central theme of the play is the hollowness of personality and the meaninglessness of what is generally called the private self. In *The Elder Statesman*, there is the echo of *The Waste Land*: the reminiscences of the meaninglessness, dryness and insanity of the modern life."[33]

The theme of sin and expatiation which is the burden of Eliot's plays has been presented in *The Elder Statesman* in its barest possible outline. "The spirit of *Everyman* who gains his spiritual freedom through confession in the medieval Morality

Everyman is present in Lord Claverton. Eliot has, however, admirably transformed the morality abstractions into the convincing pattern of a naturalistic drama."[34]

Of course, the individual's refinement was Eliot's main concern, which was the driving force behind all his plays. He deeply desired the salvation of the individual soul, as he wrote in *The Criterion*: "What ultimately matters is the salvation of the individual soul. You may not like this principle, but if you abjure it, you will probably in the end get something that you like less." By this Eliot did not mean that everybody should become a saint or a martyr. But he wanted everyone to strive for purity and holiness after having come out of one's narrow circle of pride, ego and superiority. The most important principle that unifies all his plays is the principle of humility—a quality that is most important for the salvation of the individual and the society.[35]

In *The Elder Statesman*, Eliot examines his theme of 'guilt and expatiation' in terms of Sophocles' version of *Oedipus at Colonus*. Lord Claverton, an elder statesman, faces his past and its hollowness, after a lifelong evasion. He has lived a life of illusion and unreality. His public reputation has blurred his inner vision. In the final analysis of the thematic impact, Lord Claverton expiates and cleans himself and seeks refuge under the ceremonial peace of "the great beech tree."[36] His sins change meaning by penitence.

"Like *Oedipus at Colonus*, *The Elder Statesman* depicts the tragic predicament of an old man. Led by his daughter, Antigone, Oedipus takes refuge in the grove at Colonus. Similarly Lord Claverton seeks refuse in Badgley Court—his final resting place. And like Oedipus too, Lord Claverton is attended by his daughter and visited by a son who is in trouble and wants his help and with whom he has a scene of bitter recrimination. But while in Sophocles, the recognition springs from supernatural knowledge, in Eliot this knowledge comes intuitively."[37] In *The Elder Statesman* Gomez and Mrs. Carghill want to restore Lord Claverton to his past associations, just like the people of Thebes who want to carry off Oedipus to the homeland. The meeting between Lord Claverton and Michael reminds us of Oedipus' meeting with Polyneices. The same bitterness attends upon their encounter. Lord Claverton finally disappears from the stage with the same message of love to his daughter, as does Oedipus towards the end of the Greek play. Lord Claverton's death like Oedipus' is symbolic of the well being of those whom he leaves behind. We hear Charles say to Monica about the spiritual influence of her father's death:

"It is not at all strange,
The dead has poured out a blessing on the living."[38]

However, according to E. Martin Browne, "...the intention of the two are totally different."[39] "In Oedipus we do not have a case of split personality as we have in Lord Claverton. Oedipus is a whole man, who belongs to an age, which holds certain firm convictions about the nature of man.... Eliot is writing in an age of shifting sand in which man yesterday and man today are two different beings. His protagonist is a hollow man, who wears a 'public mask,' under which he fears that there is no identity. The process of his play is by daring to strip off the mask, to find the identity."[40] According to Carol H. Smith, "This striping off of false masks before death makes up the chief dramatic action of the play."[41]

Thus the major symbol in the play is the *mask*. And Eliot has expanded his conception of the play as the transparent mask meant to be looked through, for the religious meanings, which lie behind the dramatic events. The stripping off of the false masks before death makes up the chief dramatic action of the play, which is achieved by his confession to his daughter and his acceptance of the power of forgiveness and love. As D.E. Jones succinctly puts it, "final words to daughter might serve as an epigraph to Eliot's play"[42]:

"One word
Makes all the difficulties disappear
That word is Love."[43]

The plot provides almost playfully, external and stageable points of reference for this essentially interior drama. In a Hamlet-like soliloquy, Claverton speaks of the savagely unforgiving judge within him and of the enacting nature of the inner self, which sits as judge over one's own action:

"What is this self inside us, this silent observer
Severe and speechless critic, who can terrorise us
And urge us on to futile activity
And in the end, judge us still more severely
For the errors into which his own reproaches drove us?"[44]

In Michael he finds a ghost of his former self. As Mrs. Carghill points out: "He is the picture of you, Richard/ As you were once."[45]

Thus hiding private failure behind public success, the hero learns to live with his ghosts—himself more than a ghost. The ghosts of the past are real people, not just objectifications of elements in Lord Claverton's conscience. They exist in their own right, but they are also reminders for him of the wrongs he has committed. Finally, cherished by his daughter Monica and rejected by his son, he dies under a beech tree, having exorcised the shadows of moral turpitude; inward fears though outwardly represented by two figures from his past. "Perhaps, the most interesting creations in *The Elder Statesman* are the characters of Gomez and Mrs. Carghill, the 'ghosts' of Lord Claverton's buried past. They are, the figures of a shady underworld, at once symbolic and real.... They are the ghosts of their old selves, Fred Culverwell and Maisie Montjoy, so is Lord Claverton of the long forgotten Dick Ferry."[46]

"Like the Tempters in *Murder in the Cathedral* and the 'Eumenides' in *The Family Reunion* they significantly assist the hero to reach the final stage of illumination and self-knowledge. There is a remarkable affinity between Becket's confrontation of the Tempters and Lord Claverton's encounter with the 'Ghosts' of his past. These ghosts bear a close resemblance to the 'Furies' of *The Family Reunion*.... The 'Furies' that haunt Harry, at first appear as the harrowing specters of his own sense of guilt, and he tries to flee away from their tormenting presence, but later facing them bravely he recognizes in them the liberating 'angels' of his life.... Undoubtedly, the 'ghosts' of *The Elder Statesman* are Eliot's modifications of the 'Eumenides' of *The Family*

The Elder Statesman

Reunion.... The difficulties of dramatic representation of the 'Eumenides' in the realistic theatre have urged Eliot to devise a more acceptable version of the same in his last play."[47] The 'Furies' in *The Family Reunion* appear as supernatural agents or spiritual symbols, but the 'Ghosts' of *The Elder Statesman* move about and act as familiar figures of society.

Grover Smith while analyzing the use of 'ghosts' in *The Elder Statesman* writes about Eliot's obsession with 'ghosts.' "It is interesting to think how often Eliot has written about ghosts. When Gerontion sadly muses, '*I have no ghosts*', he is at least haunted in mind by the enduring past; and Tiresias, looking into the mirror of his memory, sees reflected a throng of unquiet wraiths. *Burnt Norton* has its unactualised presences in the rose garden, *East Coker* its ancestral phantoms espied in a deserted village, *Little Gidding* its familiar compound ghost. The specters in *The Rock* are conventional, but those in *Murder in the Cathedral* are ambiguous and strange. The Eumenides of *The Family Reunion* pass from the mythology into supernaturalism. Lavinia in *The Cocktail Party* rises from the past as from the tomb, to be reunited with her husband." Thus Eliot had been using these devices much before he realized their dramatic value. He conjured up the ghosts to reveal the dead past. Their secret lies in the meaning attached by Eliot to tradition, through which one tries to understand the 'self' that is rooted there. "*The Elder Statesman*, like some of the earlier plays, reveals man's dead past; it confronts him with the living successors to the selves of a man and woman with whom his own dead self was discreditably involved." Grover Smith also cites how Eliot's use of 'ghosts' in *The Elder Statesman* is analogous to the *Turn of The Screw* by Henry James, who suggests in his Haunted Tales how "the true mystery of a ghost is bound up with the nature of the perceiver. A ghost is more than something seen, it is something interpreted; and the interpreter is always governed by his understanding and his moral awareness, and hence his self-knowledge." Then finally Grover Smith concludes how "*The Elder Statesman* blends a Jamesian concern for understanding with a Puritan anxiety about guilt.... The two 'ghosts' in the play are harmless provided the hero purifies his own soul. Achieving contrition, he holds them at bay. When death comes to Claverton himself, it is made tranquil by his daughter's compassionate love."[48]

The dramatic action of *The Elder Statesman* is adjusted according to the needs of the surface action, but the basic concepts remain the same, as developed earlier in Eliot's other plays. Lord Claverton must confess the hollowness of his public postures before he can think of attaining self-knowledge. The state of spiritual vacuum he suffers from, is best expressed in his own words which before death he compares himself to a passenger who is waiting for the train that never comes:

"It's just like sitting in an empty waiting room
In a railway station on a branch line,
After the last train, after all the other passengers
Have left. And the booking office is closed
And the porters have gone. What am I waiting for
In a cold and empty room before an empty grate?
For no one. For nothing."[49]

These words beautifully describe Lord Claverton's loneliness and his haunting sense of fear from the ghosts of his shady past. His "deeply poignant confession of the emptiness that grips his mind so relentlessly at once reminds us of a passage from *East Coker* which describes memorably the inner hollowness of those busy and prestigious professionals."[50]

"O dark dark dark. They all go into the dark,
The vacant interstellar spaces, the vacant into the vacant,
The captains, merchant bankers, eminent men of letters.
The generous patrons of art, the statesmen and the rulers,
Distinguished civil servants, chairmen of many committees,
Industrial lords and petty contractors, all go into the dark"[51]

Then as the play proceeds further Michael presents before him a prototype of his past failings and of his deceptive life. He, therefore, makes a frantic effort to save Michael from those mistakes, which he himself has committed. But this does not resolve the crisis. Hence he has finally to accept and face the reality and accept the ameliorating influence exercised by human love. Significantly, love sends 'the fugitive'[52] back to reality. Naturally by confessing his failures Claverton prepares himself to face the reality as it is. Thus at the thematic level *The Elder Statesman* deals with human love as the revelation of divinity in ordinary life.

"Both the tone and structure of *The Elder Statesman* are carefully arranged to stress the importance of love in the process of self-knowledge. The author opens the play with a love scene between Monica and her suitor, Charles. The developing relationship between the young lovers is used throughout the play to exert an emotional control over the other events and to reflect the effect of these events upon their love.... Their conversation states the theme, which is developed throughout the stages of Lord Claverton's spiritual re-education. They recognize the transforming power of love."[53] The love of Monica and Charles is meant to exemplify the positive and beneficial power of love, while Lord Claverton's unawakened state before his act of contrition exemplifies the destructive and malignant power of love perverted and betrayed. Lord Claverton finally realizes the power of love just before his death when he says:

"I've just now had the illumination
Of knowing what love is."[54]

He blesses the lovers as he leaves them, and the action of the play concludes as it began, with a love scene between Monica and Charles in which they face together the knowledge and meaning of Lord Claverton's death. They realize that the love they feel for each other will be their salvation, for it will insure the preservation of their Christian identities; they will find in human love the reflection of divine love. In Lord Claverton's suffering and death they find rebirth as "a new person. Who is you and me together."[55] The play ends as Charles says, "The dead has poured out a blessing on the living."[56]

The imagery of death and rebirth is emphatic in the close of *The Elder Statesman* when Lord Claverton says:

"And in becoming no one, I begin to live.
It is worthwhile dying, to find out what life is."[57]

"The structure of the play is again based on the pattern of ritual cure.... Through his daughter's saving love and his admission of guilt, he is purged through death of his mortality and made ready for his rebirth as spirit."[58]

Hugh Kenner in *The Invisible Poet*[59] finds that his daughter Monica, who seems to have stepped into the play from *Marina*, tells her lover that love has been the shield protecting both of them. They are not the persons we think we see, but "conscious of a new person, who is you and me together"[60] Her father, we are given to understand dies offstage: ("He is under the beech tree. It is quiet and cold there."[61]) Her last words are addressed to Charles:

"I feel utterly secure
In you. I am a part of you. Now take me to my father."[62]

As if to draw particular attention to the merger of personal and universal meanings in *The Elder Statesman*, Eliot has included in the printed version of the play a dedication to his wife Valerie which expresses the same idea in more personal terms:

"The words (of the play) mean what they say, but some have a further meaning.

For you and me only."[63]

The unity which the poet hopes to achieve between private and public experience is thus appropriate to the play's theme.[64]

M.C. Bradbrook also affirms how thematically *The Elder Statesman* recalls Marina in its joyous affirmation of the grace transmitted through human love. "The transparent valedictory quality of this play gives it a distinction, which is not that of a work for the stage; all the characters are disembodied from the start. Monica, the only one to achieve a complete absolution of solitude, a complete capacity for love finds that in her the 'obstinate silent self' who is the unspeaking director of ordinary persons has been replaced by 'a love that's lived in, but not looked at'; and 'this love is silent.' Monica is the only character permitted to reach the emotional level of poetry."[65]

As in the earlier plays, here also Eliot has combined the pagan myth with Christian values in the 20th century perspective.

As Carol H. Smith says, "For the Christian...there is that perpetual living in paradox. You must lose your life to save it. One has to be otherworldly and yet deeply responsible for the affairs of this world. One must preserve a capacity for enjoying the things of this world such as love and affection."[66] It is love that sends the fugitive back home to reality. "The symbolism of death and rebirth has been powerfully presented in the play. Lord Claverton's almost Buddha like meditation under the beech tree leads to his spiritual illumination on the eve of death. His physical death is a prelude to purification and rebirth and his ultimate union with God."[67]

Thus, *The Elder Statesman* is a play not so much about Claverton as about Everyman. It resembles a Morality play both in respect of structure as well as versification. Eliot is writing Moralities in the idiom of his own times and in his own idiosyncratic way about eternal values. Like an ancient Morality play, *The Elder Statesman* uses a simple and quickly grasped situation presented by uncomplicated characters to speak profound and difficult things about human spirit. It is his effort to do this which gives to all Eliot's dramas a timeless and placeless quality.[68]

In this play, however, there is no formal use of the chorus, which Eliot had abandoned for good. However as already noted, the Hamlet-like soliloquies of Claverton and the incorporation of a novel machinery in the form of ghosts, the chorus almost peeps from behind the curtain. Monica, who is instrumental in stripping off the mask and in teaching him the lessons of love, also performs a powerful choric function.

The play opens with Monica and Charles talking to each other about the love that they have for each other. This introduces the central theme of the play and suggests the role of Love in human life. As Charles says:

"Your words seem to come
From very far away. Yet very near. You are changing me
And I am changing you."[69]

And further goes on to suggest how love unites the two souls:

"And how much of me is you?
I'm not the same person as a moment ago.
What do the words mean now—*I* and *You*?"[70]

This in itself is a choric function wherein the chorus suggests what the play is going to be about. In this respect we find Monica and Charles playing the role of the chorus together, wherein Monica plays the role of the leader of the chorus and Charles as subsidiary member of the choric team. Eliot has given them a dual role. They are characters of the play and are equally involved in the action. On the other hand they many times seem detached from the play making independent comments and moral reflections. They sometimes speak of their "private world" and sometimes they say "Now we are in the public world."[71]

While Monica reflects on certain human problems and emotions in general we feel as if the chorus itself is speaking to the audience. Look at one of her remarks:

"Envy is everywhere.
Who is without envy/ And most people
Are unaware or unashamed of being envious.
It's all we can ask if compassion and wistfulness...
And tenderness, Charles! Are mixed with envy."[72]

Then after the Prologue when it comes to Episodes and Stasimon, we find that there are actually three episodes in the play—firstly Lord Claverton's encounter with Gomez, the first ghost of his past and then in the second Act Claverton meets Mrs. Carghill, the second ghost of his past and then in the third episode he meets his own son who happens to be his prototype or in this respect may be called his own ghost. On all these occasions we find Monica interacting with the protagonist and making her own comments, which are definitely choric in spirit. Finally then in the Exodus we find after the departure of the hero or his presumed death, Monica and Charles make their final comment on the basic theme and action of the play moralizing on the importance of Love in human life. At the personal level Charles says:

"So that now we are conscious of a new person
Who is you and me together."[73]

And then Monica also feels:
> "Fixed in the certainty of love unchanging
> I feel utterly secure
> In you; I am a part of you."[74]

She has already convinced her father Lord Claverton about the power of love. His cure is wrought by the spiritual agency of his daughter's saving love. All this goes to prove that Monica and Charles play the same role that chorus used to play in Greek tragedy and Eliot has deftly used them as such.

However, in *The Elder Statesman*, we again find Eliot moving back to a more lyrical surface and he uses poetry as a dramatic tool and infuses into the fable all the dramatic excitement. With the verbal beauty of the dialogues, he has been able to recoup his losses and yet not lose his gains. "Nevertheless, Eliot's endeavour to create a new genre which would be both dramatically compelling and spiritually profound in terms and meaningful to the modern age is a goal which must be endorsed, especially when it has been espoused by one of the major poetic talents of the 20th century."[75] Still, however, with his long strides to meet the audience at their ground, Eliot could never abandon poetry, which continued to form the very soul of his communicative mode. This poetic quality of his plays in spite of the thinning out of the verse compensates for the absence of the formal chorus in the play. But the chorus has never been completely absent. Its function is either performed by certain choric characters like Monica in *The Elder Statesman*, who is also the mouthpiece of the dramatist. Such characters provide a running commentary and also play the role of *Helpers* in guiding the *Blinds* towards purgation and self-realisation, playing the role of the auxiliary chorus. Hamlet-like soliloquies of the hero also project the inner permutations of the protagonist, a function which was many times allotted to the Chorus. Thus it can be safely concluded that in the later plays of Eliot the chorus may not be physically present on the stage, it definitely standing in the wings.

NOTES AND REFERENCES

1. Smith, Carol H. 1963. *T.S. Eliot's Dramatic Theory and Practice*. London: Oxford University Press. 217-18.

2. Eliot, T.S. 1969. *The Complete Poems and Plays of T.S. Eliot.* London: Faber and Faber. 530.
3. *Ibid.* 536.
4. *Ibid.*
5. *Ibid.* 540.
6. *Ibid.* 541.
7. Smith, Carol H. 1963. *T.S. Eliot's Dramatic Theory and Practice.* London: Oxford University Press. 231-32.
8. Eliot, T.S. 1969. *The Complete Poems and Plays of T.S. Eliot.* London: Faber and Faber. 550-51.
9. *Ibid.* 551.
10. *Ibid.* 553.
11. *Ibid.* 555.
12. *Ibid.*
13. *Ibid.* 559.
14. *Ibid.* 561.
15. *Ibid.* 561-62.
16. *Ibid.* 522.
17. *Ibid.* 565.
18. *Ibid.* 568.
19. *Ibid.* 569.
20. *Ibid.* 572.
21. *Ibid.* 582.
22. Sarkar, Subhas. 2006. *T.S. Eliot—The Dramatist.* Delhi: Atlantic Publishers & Distributors (P) Ltd. 251.
23. Smith, Carol H. 2006. *T.S. Eliot's Dramatic Theory and Practice.* London: Oxford University Press. 227-28.
24. Eliot, T.S. 1969. *The Complete Poems and Plays of T.S. Eliot.* London: Faber and Faber. 583.
25. *Ibid.*
26. Sarkar, Subhas. 2006. *T.S. Eliot—The Dramatist.* New Delhi: Atlantic Publishers & Distributors (P) Ltd. 251.
27. *Ibid.* 251-52.
28. Eliot, T.S. 1969. *The Complete Poems and Plays of T.S. Eliot.* London: Faber and Faber. 573.
29. *Ibid.* 581.
30. *Ibid.* 583.

31. Sarkar, Sunil Kumar. 2000. *T.S. Eliot—Poetry, Plays and Prose*. New Delhi: Atlantic Publishers & Distributors (P) Ltd. 211-12.
32. Eliot, T.S. 1969. *The Complete Poems and Plays of T.S. Eliot*. London: Faber and Faber. 540.
33. Sarkar, Sunil Kumar. 2000. *T.S. Eliot—Poetry, Plays and Prose*. New Delhi: Atlantic Publishers & Distributors (P) Ltd. 202.
34. Sarkar, Subhas. 2006. *T.S. Eliot—The Dramatist*. New Delhi: Atlantic Publishers & Distributors (P) Ltd. 252.
35. Titus, T.K. 2001. *A Critical Study of T.S. Eliot's Works*. New Delhi: Atlantic Publishers & Distributors (P) Ltd. 114.
36. Eliot, T.S. 1969. *The Complete Poems and Plays of T.S. Eliot*. London: Faber and Faber. 583.
37. Singh, Parwati. 1988. *Character and Symbol in the Plays of T.S. Eliot*. Delhi: Capital Publishing House. 133.
38. Eliot, T.S. 1969. *The Complete Poems and Plays of T.S. Eliot*. London: Faber and Faber. 583.
39. Singh, Parwati. 1988. *Character and Symbol in the Plays of T.S. Eliot*. Delhi: Capital Publishing House. 135.
40. *Ibid.* 136.
41. Smith, Carol H. 1963. *T.S. Eliot's Dramatic Theory and Practice*. London: Oxford University Press. 216.
42. Jones, D.E. 1960. *The Plays of T.S. Eliot*. London: Routledge & Kegan Paul. 181.
43. Lines from *Sophocles: Oedipus at Colonus*. Quoted from Jones, D.E. 1960. *The Plays of T.S. Eliot*. London: Routledge & Kegan Paul. 181.
44. Eliot, T.S. 1969. *The Complete Poems and Plays of T.S. Eliot*. London: Faber and Faber. 545.
45. *Ibid.* 562.
46. Sarkar, Subhas. 2006. *T.S. Eliot—The Dramatist*. New Delhi: Atlantic Publishers & Distributors (P) Ltd. 276.
47. *Ibid.* 253-54.
48. Smith, Grover. 2000. *T.S. Eliot's Poetry and Plays—A Study in Sources and Meaning*. Chicago: The University of Chicago Press. First Indian Reprint. Delhi: Doaba Publications. 244-45.
49. Eliot, T.S. 1969. *The Complete Poems and Plays of T.S. Eliot*. London: Faber and Faber. 530.
50. Titus, T.K. 2001. *A Critical Study of T.S. Eliot's Works*. New Delhi: Atlantic Publishers & Distributors (P) Ltd. 110.

51. Eliot, T.S. 1969. *The Complete Poems and Plays of T.S. Eliot.* London: Faber and Faber. 182.
52. *Ibid.* 560.
53. Smith, Carol H. 1963. *T.S. Eliot's Dramatic Theory and Practice.* London: Oxford University Press. 217-18.
54. *Ibid.* 581.
55. *Ibid.* 583.
56. *Ibid.*
57. *Ibid.* 582
58. Smith, Carol H. 1963. *T.S. Eliot's Dramatic Theory and Practice.* London: Oxford University Press. 233.
59. Kenner, Hugh. 1966. *The Invisible Poet—T.S. Eliot.* London: Metheun & Co. Ltd. 290.
60. Eliot, T.S. 1969. *The Complete Poems and Plays of T.S. Eliot.* London: Faber and Faber. 583.
61. *Ibid.*
62. *Ibid.*
63. *Ibid.* 522.
64. Smith, Carol H. 1963. *T.S. Eliot's Dramatic Theory and Practice.* London: Oxford University Press. 237.
65. Bradbrook, M.C. 1965. *English Dramatic Form—A History of its Development.* London: Chatto & Windus. 175.
66. Smith, Carol H. 1963. *T.S. Eliot's Dramatic Theory and Practice.* London: Oxford University Press. 214n.
67. Singh, Parwati: 1988. *Character and Symbol in the Plays of T.S. Eliot.* Delhi: Capital Publishing House. 169.
68. *Ibid.* 155.
69. Eliot, T.S. 1969. *The Complete Poems and Plays of T.S. Eliot.* London: Faber and Faber. 526.
70. *Ibid.*
71. *Ibid.*
72. *Ibid.* 529.
73. *Ibid.* 583.
74. *Ibid.*
75. Smith, Carol H. 1963. *T.S. Eliot's Dramatic Theory and Practice.* London: Oxford University Press. 239.

Conclusion

In modern English drama there has been a trend to revive the age-old convention of the chorus. Several experiments have been conducted to adapt it to suit the changing conditions of life and stage. This emergence of the chorus has been so conspicuous that whosoever goes through any of the modern plays (especially the poetical plays) is most likely to be struck by the novelty of their technique and the strikingly unique position that the chorus enjoys in them. It is, therefore, quite natural for any one to get interested in analyzing the nature, functions and structure of the chorus through the ages.

"Dramatically, the chorus can serve many purposes. It can work as a mouthpiece of the dramatist. It can expound the past, comment on the present and illuminate the future. It provides the spectator with a counterpart of himself. It presents the inside permutations of common humanity, and has the capacity to portray human situation in its relevant perspective. With its pure poetry it can transmogrify lamentation into music, horror into peace and serious into the sublime. On the negative side the chorus was deliberately dropped by many a dramatist, since they regarded it as an encumbrance."[1]

For any proper and systematic analysis of this convention in drama, we will have to trace its origin from the temples of Dionysus and its dithyrambic associations. Originally the chorus was a group of performers at a religious festival, especially fertility rites. These choral odes, which were born from an elemental dramatic rite were a sort of a communal activity, and were very popular amongst the primitive peoples. According to C.M. Bowra, these choral odes "represent an entirely communal state of mind...common consciousness, based on a common purpose."[2]

As Vaughan has also said, "In the beginning, the performances of the Greek stage, were, in truth, entirely un-dramatic. In the first instance it would seem, there were no actors at all. The chorus supplied the only personages of the piece; and the chorus acted, in the strictest sense, as a collective body, whose function was to sing hymns...often woven around the tale of some mythical or national hero in honour of Dionysus. It is manifest that we have here nothing that can be fairly be called drama. The first step away from this purely ritual performance was taken, as some critics suppose, when one member of the chorus, the leader perhaps, was detached from the rest and a kind of antiphon instituted between him and them. Such was, or may have been, the beginning of dialogue."[3] Thus by some process of grafting or symbiosis Greek tragedy acquired (or grew out of) these choral rites. These choral odes gradually developed into the Greek tragic drama wherein the chorus played a very important part. We are also told by Aristotle[4] (*Poetics* vi), that the germ of tragedy was found in the speeches delivered by the leader of the dithyramb.

In Greek tragedies, especially those of Aeschylus and Sophocles, chorus represented a group of people who served mainly as commentators on the characters and events. They added to the audience's understanding of the play by expressing traditional moral, religious, and social attitudes. This 'stage-army', says F.L. Lucas, "can expound the past, comment on the present and forebode the future. It provides the poet with a mouthpiece and the spectator with a counterpart of himself. It also forms a living foreground of the common humanity."[5]

But with the development of the dramatic art the battle of the Individual against the Group started. Thespis, it is said, had introduced the first actor; with Aeschylus came the second and with Sophocles the third—at which the Greek tragedy mysteriously stopped.[6] This gradually diminished the importance of the chorus. Its former position as a leading agent in the plot was exchanged for a passive role of a spectator.

Historically, the chorus possesses a chequered history of its development. Aeschylus and Sophocles developed the chorus to its supreme heights. But "the chorus which in Aeschylus was a

Conclusion

flexible institution, in Sophocles acquires a fixed and permanent position, and continually reappears in the same stereotyped form. It is not only curtailed in size, but also gradually loses its individuality. The utterances of the chorus now become cool, and sober reflections rather than violent personal passion. It now stands aloof from the stress and storm of the action and assumes the office of an impartial mediator. It is finally excluded from any real share in the action."[7] Thus, chorus in Sophocles is not an effective agent in the plot. Later the history of the chorus in Euripides is a history of further decline. Gradually losing power they occupy the pauses of the play with long and ornate descriptions of some legendary event and are gradually converted into musical interludes. "Chorus at last, fades like an Echo and becomes in Euripides, at times, a mere disembodied voice."[8] But at times even in his later works, Euripides restores chorus to much of its original grandeur and significance.

Then, at a later stage in history, Roman writers like Seneca although retained a chorus, yet in retaining it they carried to further limits the trend already noted in the works of Sophocles and more particularly of Euripides. The choral odes in the tragedies, some of them gifted with cold loveliness are generally unrelated, to the events narrated in the main action. Fundamentally the chorus has now become merely a purveyor of Interludes. Summing up this gradual decline F.L. Lucas has beautifully said, "The characters in Aeschylus had been colossi, and even his choruses of heroic stature; the characters of Sophocles heroic, his choruses simply human; the characters of Euripides become human, his choruses half ghosts.... After this it is only its bare, disheveled ghost that wails between the acts of the tragedies in Seneca. The chorus that once had unified plays now serves to divide them into acts."[9]

As we come down to the Middle Ages, The drama from which originated the Mysteries, Miracles and Interludes, "began in the Church, not in the theatre, in song not in spoken dialogue, in worship not in entertainment...."[10] As Lucas puts it: "From the tomb of Christ, as once perhaps of Dionysus, the drama rises again into life; again ritual becomes art. But no chorus reappears to dance down the cobbled streets of Coventry or Wakefield. The Middle Ages danced even in the churchyard itself; but their dance failed to wed their drama."[11]

Then, with the transference of the drama from the Church to the laity, regular mysteries and miracle plays began to flow in regularly, in the form of certain cycles. In the extant plays of the various cycles the choric tradition finds its place in a different form. There is the complete and conspicuous absence of the chorus in its physical form, in the drama, but the functional aspect of the chorus can be traced out here and there. These choric devices in the form of Prologue and Epilogue through which the dramatist continues to work as the conscience keeper of the community are to be found in almost all the important plays.

The Messenger in *Everyman* as also in some of the Chester plays like *The Sacrifice of ISAAC* reads out the Prologue and the Epilogue is sung by the 'Doctour' or the 'Expositor,' who expounds the moral of the performance. In the Moralities their place is also sometimes taken by one of the various characters, as Good Deeds in *Everyman*. These Prologues and Epilogues or the devices of some characters performing the choric function was later adopted by Shakespeare and other Renaissance-dramatists; but except for these unimportant choric devices in the early drama of England, we would but labour in vain to find out any other vestiges of the Greek chorus or any of its adaptations in newer form.

The Humanist and the Individualist trends during the Renaissance period, accounts for the absence of the chorus in the Elizabethan drama. It was based on the glorification of human personality and hence was not considered necessary for the expression of true tragic emotions. However, the choric function was performed either through the Prologue of the Epilogue and certain other conventions like the 'soliloquy' which do the work of the chorus in explaining the inner conflicts of the characters. Certain characters also do the same job, as that of the chorus, without being given that formal name. Then, the song element of the Shakespearean drama also compensates for the absence of the chorus by providing the lyrical element to the play, which

Conclusion

was originally one of the chief functions of the chorus. Thus in some of the earlier Elizabethan tragedies where chorus was adopted, it was simply a reproduction of the Senecan chorus.

Although the chorus is not present in most of the Elizabethan plays, yet their success lay not in resurrecting the ancient convention, but in inventing other ways of doing what it had done. For if the popular Elizabethan playwright had no chorus, on the other hand he could have on the stage at once not three characters only, but almost as many as he chose. And a single one of them, like Enobarbus in *Antony and Cleopatra* might suffice by himself to do much of the work, the chorus once performed. We have such character-choruses in other plays also, as Horatio in *Hamlet*. Then practically the Shakespearean Fool, as in *King Lear* or Touchstone in *As You Like It* or Feste in *The Winters Tale*, has always the choric function to perform. There are also some scenes in Shakespeare, which serve as a substitute for the chorus. The 'grave-digger-scene' in *Hamlet* is an example of such a technique. The soliloquy is yet another device which Renaissance dramatists use to their own advantages in analysing the inner conflicts of the character's mind. This technique had a special advantage over chorus. Then the song element in Shakespearean Drama also compensates for the absence of the chorus of providing the lyrical element in the play, which was one of the chief functions of the chorus itself.

All this is indicative of the fact that the Renaissance dramatists had developed an altogether new type of dramatic structure, different from the classical one, wherein chorus had no place. They, however, had so many other devices to compensate for the absence of this ancient convention. As F.L. Lucas says, "Where the Greek chorus served as a foil, a type of common humanity beside the heroic figures of legend, the Shakespearean stage has its meaner characters, its citizens, its crowds, its clowns. Where the Greek chorus provided a lyric relief for tragic tension, Elizabethan dramatists have on the one hand the laughter of their fools, on the other the lyric beauty of their stage-songs and the poetry they can put in the mouth of almost any character, however sordid or villainous."[12]

The credit, however, goes to Milton for reviving the Greek form of drama with the chorus as the central convention. In *Samson Agonistes* the chorus occupies an important place in the structure of the drama. It is a sharer in the action of the play. In grandeur and loftiness *Samson Agonistes* approaches the Aeschylean drama. In the conduct of his chorus Milton is even superior to Euripides, whose choruses indulge in sententious maxims and wordy declamations, too often irrelevant and wide off the mark.

The chorus of *Samson Agonistes* is, like its Sophoclean prototype. Here although the chorus does play some part in the hero's regeneration yet this influence is comparatively slight. Instead of comforting Samson, they are soon led to echo his despair. The trait is thoroughly Sophoclean. So the other functions of the chorus, like representing the common aspects of morality, consoling the afflicted hero, and cautioning against oppression and finally acting as a spokesman of the dramatist, are however on a feebler note.

After Milton, for a very long time, the chorus was not present even in an indirect way, because the drama was becoming more and more secularized and prosaic in style with a great amount of social criticism and comedy at the expense of individual follies as in the Comedies of Manners and Sentiments. In some of the serious plays, however, as in Mason's *Elfrida,* there is a chorus of British virgins and in *Eractacus* a chorus of Druids and Bards. The conspicuous absence of the chorus in this age is also due to the fact that the plays in the 18th century had cut themselves off, from the ritual atmosphere from which emanated the Greek and the Elizabethan drama.

However, during this period, the chorus was going over to the operas and musical comedies. In the operas chorus became one of the most attractive features providing spectacle and musicality. The operatic chorus almost fulfilled the Greek Conventions, and they progressed greatly during the Romantic period. Important among them are Mozart's *Don Giovanni* and the operas of Handel and J.S. Bach. The chorus is also present in the light operas like Gay's *Baeggar's Opera* which is one of the outstanding achievements of the English stage in the early 18th century.

On the continent also the attraction for the chorus was quite great. It was used, with great enthusiasm in the Italian, Spanish, French and German literatures. Tasso introduced it in *Torismondo* (1586) and Lope de Vega (1562–1635) in his *Aranco Domado*. It also occurs in French literature in Racine, who has used it in *Esther* (1689) and in *Athalie* (1691). Then it also appears in the works of the great German dramatist Schiller in his *Bride of Messina* (1804), "which in respect of form—the retention, for example, of the chorus—adheres much more closely to the Athenian model than anything produced by Goethe."[13] Besides these significant plays there are a number of other plays wherein this convention has been successfully used.

In England, it was then left to the Romantic poets like Shelley and Byron to think of the chorus on a Greek model. There is a chorus of Swinish Multitude in *Oedipus Tyrannus* and of abstract spirits, like Furies, Spirits and Hours in the *Prometheus Unbound*; and also in *Hellas*, we find a chorus of Greek captive women. Similarly Byron also introduced a chorus of Earth Spirits and Mortals in his mystery *Heaven and Earth*. Thus the chorus of these Romantic poets is the chorus of abstract spirits and symbolic figures. Had they been substituted with concrete characters they would have succeeded in giving us a new form—workable on the stage. Still, however, their chorus propounds the personal philosophies of the poets and gives expression to their lyricism.

The Victorian poets too experimented with drama. But they were the sort of plays that would not 'act.' They were far too 'literary.' Matthew Arnold and Swinburne evinced a keen interest in Greek drama. There is a chorus in Swinburne's *Atalanta in Calydon* (1865) and in *Erectheus* (1876) there is Chorus of Athenian Elders. Then we have Mrs. Browning's *Drama of Exile* (1844), which has the Chorus of Eden Spirits and Invisible Angels. But the more important work of this age is Arnold's *Merope* (1858) which has got a Chorus of Messonian Maidens and the choric odes are strophic and antistrophic. In the preface to this play, Arnold has also provided significant comments on the need for reviving the chorus in English Drama.

But the most significant attempts in reviving the chorus have, however, been made in modern times by the 'poets of the theatre' in the field of poetic drama. Symbolists like Sturge Moore, John Masefield and James Elroy Flecker made significant attempts in this direction. W.B. Yeats in his great effort to revive the poetic drama devised various types of choruses with dancers and adapted the Noh technique in his plays. Gordon Bottomley also used the chorus of curtain folders following Yeats's experiments. Then chorus has also been a stock element in all the religious plays of Masefield, Bottomley and others.

In the tradition of the poetic plays, also comes the great modern master—T.S. Eliot, whose contribution in this field is of immense value. Eliot explored the drama of the Elizabethans and the Ancients and put into it a new sense of renaissance wonder and greatness. He enlarged the scope of the verse drama and gave the poetic drama a new dimension and a new medium. He also developed a verse form suitable for contemporary situations and revitalized the theatre of the day.[14]

Eliot while adopting the Greek pattern of the chorus was fairly alive to the relevant aspects of its application. He admitted that in making use of the chorus, he did not intend to copy Greek drama, nor did he aim at using it too frequently. He gave the chorus an entirely new dimension by making it an integral part of the play. His major achievement, therefore, is the way he developed appropriate method to integrate the subject matter of his themes with the dramatic structure of his plays.

Eliot is supposed to have made his debut as a dramatist in *Sweeney Agonistes* (1926), wherein he tries to fuse the ancient and the modern together to present a powerful piece of dramatic art. The theme of a spiritual pilgrimage has been deftly woven by T.S. Eliot into the texture of a poetic play in which myth and ritual of ancient Greece have been woven with hectic, artificial sensual life of the modern fashionable society. He revived the chorus on the Aeschylean model where the Choric and the

Conclusion

Histrionic elements were held in a balance and fused into an organic whole. In *Sweeney* the chorus is represented by characters belonging to the sensual world—Wauchope, Horsfall, Klipstein, Drumpacker, Snow and Swarts who rejoice only in their physical and sensual existence and try to elude the uninitiated soul of Doris away from his spiritual guide.

The chorus in *Sweeney* forms an inseparable part of the play and helps in advancing its main action. It plays a positive role in depicting the conflict and the dénouement. In the beginning the chorus expresses its agreement with the 'copulation theme'[15] but at the end endorses the substance of the final 'purgatorial Ode,'[16] which culminates into a melodramatic close when the full chorus presents a nightmare depicting the knocking of the Fate at the door of the penitent.[17] The fear of the Unknown has been beautifully depicted in the melodramatic 'hoo-ha'[18] of the concluding chorus.

In the field of language also, *Sweeney Agonistes*, anticipates Eliot's later plays in its skilful adaptation of the modern speech rhythm in dramatic dialogues and its clever use into the choric form. Eliot's chief concern was to come to terms with the speech of the time. So, using chorus to voice the communal feelings, he also uses the language of the common man. While incorporating the incantatory rhythms of the jazz songs and the conversational tones of the telephonic dialogues, Eliot seems to have combined the music of the twentieth century with the technique of the Greek drama.

Eliot states that the conditions of modern life have altered our 'perceptions of rhythms.' Hence he has rejected the conventional tones in his plays. Thus we find that in *Sweeney Agonistes* "the poet has injected into his music hall rhythms, the full force of an intense spiritual experience, so that the silly songs frequently become ritual formulae charged with philosophical or religious allusions."[19] The alchemy of Eliot's art transforms the parody of the Shakespearean song (Under the Greenwood tree) into a powerful living reality. It is the Metaphysical's way of joining together the trivial and the serious.

The Rock (1934), a pageant play, is Eliot's next excursion into drama. Although here Eliot was writing under the direction of E. Martin Browne, who wrote the scenario. Eliot in his Prefatory Note to the play owns the authorship of all the ten choruses, which embody a spiritual message of Christian theology along with his mystic revelations of the Eternity. The episodes of the play are loosely linked together by the chorus.

The chorus comprising of seven men and ten women, emphasize not only their own personality, but also that of the entire ecclesiastical system governing the institution of the church. Wearing half masks and stiff robes, they speak with the voice of the poet. The members of the chorus are not individualized and they do not have any character of their own. They merely serve as the voice piece of the author's views and represent some of the best meditative poetry that Eliot was to develop in the Quartets. Although it hardly meets Eliot's test for a religious play "that should be able to hold the interest, to arouse the excitement of people who are not religious, nor through the very nature of its inception could it possibly rise to his far more exacting demand of creating an indisseverable double pattern of poetry and drama."[20]

There is a complete absence of dramatic conflict in the play and the choruses are also devoid of any dramatic emotion. They represent a number of different poetic moods; occasionally a devotional mood, but more often an elegiac mood of mourning for the wholeness of the vision now lost to the society or sometimes a satiric mood in which the superficiality of the modern life is castigated.

The other change, brought about by the chorus of *The Rock*, is the final freeing of the verse from the counting of syllables. Eliot has broken the blank verse tradition of syllables by going at once backward and forward. He has gone back to the basis established by the medieval poets of a fixed number of stresses in the line, without any fixed number of syllables. He has gone forward to meet the development of prose rhythm by the inclusion of a very long, sweepingly rhythmic line having six or eight stresses, but still a part of the verse structure. Thus a form of verse, more varied than any before, was placed at the service of the theatre by the chorus of *The Rock*.

Despite its weaknesses, *The Rock* is an important stage in the development of Eliot's dramatic career. It prepared him for his coming masterpiece—*Murder in the Cathedral* (1935), where the Women of Canterbury provide a powerful chorus to the play. But as John Peter says, their position in the play is ambivalent. "At one stage, they are simply the poor women of Canterbury, at another level...transparently more than their natural selves. Like their equivalent in Greek tragedy they present a commentary on the action, anticipating and preparing us for developments, rousing us with their passionate dithyrambs, to participate wholeheartedly in the emotional crises that arise, supplying the action with a background that is, like music all pervasive."[21] They also give expression to the communal feeling which usually runs deeper than individual feeling, though not usually so articulate. Both the beginning and end of the action in the play are conducted by the chorus. Through its reactions to the event of the martyrdom of Thomas—through its opposition and its final reconciliation, the tension and the powerful atmosphere is maintained. Without the chorus, the plot would have suffered a lot of suffocation and strangulation.

It is with these choruses that Eliot is poetically most successful. As Helen Gardner also says, "The greatest drama of the play is to be found where the greatest poetry lies—in the choruses."[22] It intensifies the emotional consequences of the action and provides for the emotional release of the tension. The chorus in *Murder in the Cathedral* is perhaps the greatest thing in a great play. There is nothing else like them in English. In fact, we have to go back to Greek tragedy to find choral writings with which to compare the best of them.

The choruses in *Murder in the Cathedral* owe much to the rhythm of Biblical verses with its simplicity of syntax, emphatic repetitions and rhythmical variety. Choral metres are different from the metres of dialogue, because when many voices speak together subtle modulations are not possible and choral speeches have to be emphatic, regular and loud. So the choric chants differ from the verse of the hero, the Knights, the Priests or the Tempters.

Thus with the fusion of the elements of the Christian drama of the Middle Ages with the Pre-Christian drama of the Greeks, Eliot has evolved an entirely original form. As D.E. Jones says, "Not only is the full throated chorus of Greek tragedy restored, but its original function is enlarged in the light of the Christian liturgy."[23] As Williams Raymond observes, "The function is merged in a larger method, for which the tradition lives; the chorus becomes a link between ritual and believers; chorus is choir; the articulate voice of the body of worshippers."[24]

Besides the Women of Canterbury, who constitute the formal chorus, all the other characters, except the protagonist, who stand in groups also have a choric function to perform, because each one of them represents the viewpoint of a particular group. And as D.E. Jones says, "The elements of spiritual conflict in Thomas are objectified in a massive antiphony of three choral groups."[25]

Thus as T.S. Eliot himself says, "The introduction of a chorus of excited and sometimes hysterical women, reflecting in their emotions the significance of action, helped wonderfully... a poet writing for the first time for the stage is much more at home in choral verse than in dramatic dialogue. This I felt sure was something I could do, and perhaps the dramatic weaknesses would be somewhat covered up by the cries of women. The use of a chorus strengthened the power and concealed the defects of my theatrical techniques. For this reason I decided that next time I would try to integrate the chorus more closely into the play."[26]

Thus, as already envisaged by Eliot, in *The Family Reunion*, he has shown some rethinking in the use of the chorus. Perhaps he realized that in *Murder in the Cathedral*, he depended rather heavily on the assistance of the chorus. Therefore he decided to relegate chorus to a secondary position and to integrate it more closely into the central design of the play. The chorus in *The Family Reunion* actually consists of Harry's uncles and aunts, who have also been assigned separate roles, quite different from their collective characters. The characters of the chorus in *The Family Reunion* are flat characters, but they have also been individualized by their different reactions to the hero's dilemma and by the characteristic verse pattern each is given to speak. They are stock English types, slightly caricatured. From time to time, they draw together as if to find safety in numbers and voice their fear of the Unknown.

The chorus of *The Family Reunion* is no more there in its conventional sense of "illuminating the action," but on the other hand it creates a relative feeling of inability to discern what is happening on the stage. As Mathiessen points out, "They are unlike the usual Greek chorus in that their role is not to illuminate the action but to express the baffled inability to understand what is happening."[27] They 'stand like guilty conspirators, waiting for some revelation when the hidden shall be exposed.'[28] Thus unlike the tremendous emotional appeal provided by the chorus in *Murder in the Cathedral*, the chorus in *The Family Reunion* have a limited role to play.

Eliot, himself, regards this device as "very unsatisfactory" since it creates problems for the actors and also obstructs the proper growth of action. The major hurdle is the transition form the individual role to the role of the chorus. "It is," says Eliot, "a very difficult transition to accomplish."[29] According to Frederick Lumley, "The experiment of using, as chorus, four minor characters, whose sudden ritualistic chant seem quite out of harmony with their previous roles, can only be described as embarrassing."[30]

Besides the formal chorus, Eliot also adopts certain dramatic machinery to play the role of auxiliary chorus. Sometimes he introduces certain characters to fulfil the desired function. As he has himself confessed, "My intention was to have one character whose sensibility and intelligence should be on the plane of the most sensitive and intelligent members of the audience; his speech should be addressed to them as much as to the other personages in the play—or rather should be addressed to the latter, who were to be material, literal minded and visionless, with the consciousness of being overheard by the former."[31] Sometimes these characters play the role of Guardians with

Guardianship becoming a special machinery of the plot. As instruments of a higher power, the Guardians contrive a good deal of action of the play. In this way symbolism becomes highly functional and contrariwise their manipulation of the plot assumes a metaphorical significance and suggests the way Divine Providence works in society. Williams Raymond also indicates that they are agents of salvation, not of an individual only but often of a group or even of the society at large.

Thus, besides the supernatural machinery of the Eumenides, the Guardians in *The Family Reunion* also help in advancing the action of the play by guiding the protagonist towards spiritual realisation. So as D.E. Jones says, "Agatha acts as an auxiliary chorus, because the function of the main chorus is to represent obtuse humanity, someone is needed to interpret the action more perceptibly and Agatha is best suited to do that."[32]

Thus while the formal chorus in *The Family Reunion* provide nothing like the tremendous emotional release of the previous play, the emotional release here occurs much more in the quasi-soliloquies or the lyrical duets between Harry and Mary and between Harry and Agatha, where the characters move into a state of communion and share experience at the deepest level of being.

After *The Family Reunion*, Eliot finally decides to drop the use of the formal chorus in his subsequent plays. But while he abandons the chorus, he definitely adopts compensatory devices which fill the vacuum so caused, and the choric function continues to be performed by some device or the other.

One such device is the use of the mythical method by Eliot in his plays. A myth, in this context, is the first logical mode of expression by the primitive man and gives a symbolic significance to human experience. To the dramatist they provide the frame of reference within which he can formulate or define a structure of meaning. It provides the writer an analogy to achieve suggestive evocation of deeper meaning. It also establishes a continuous parallel between the past and the present. Thus by the use of the mythical method Eliot has been able to create a kind of double pattern in the drama and the audience might discern one meaning at the surface level while the myth might invoke another meaning at the deeper level. Thus with all its symbolism and suggestivity the mythical method works as a latent chorus in the plays of Eliot.

Moreover, in the plays of Eliot we also find an integration of drama into the framework of the ritual atmosphere. The ritual role of the serio-comic, symbolic *Cook-Doctor* as a spiritual agent is yet another type of dramatic machinery used by Eliot in almost all his plays for spiritual regeneration and self-realization. Beginning with Pereira in *Sweeney Agonistes*. Dr. Warburton in *The Family Reunion*, Sir Henry Harcourt Reilly in *The Cocktail Party*, Eggerson in *The Confidential Clerk* and the Doctor who orders Lord Claverton to the Sanitorium in *The Elder Statesman* in a series of such characters who present a ritual background and succinctly perform the role of the chorus with a mask on.

The Eumenides in *The Family Reunion* and the ghosts in *The Elder Statesman*, represent the supernatural machinery to guide the action of the play and to lead the protagonist to the desired dénouement. As M.C. Bradbrook says, "Ghosts and messengers from another world appear everywhere—Pereira on the telephone, an ominous threatening visitant; Thomas's tempters, from his past life; Harry's Furies; Celia, and by way of parody, Lavinia's aunt; Mrs. Guzzard, with the news of Colby's dead father; Gomez and Maisie."[33] All these characters and the supernatural machinery play a powerful role in guiding the action of the plot and thus play a choric role. Here we find the chorus peeping from behind the curtain.

The machinery of Guardianship, which works as an instrument of higher power to guide the action of the play is constantly found present in almost all the plays of Eliot. characters like Sweeney in *Sweeney Agonistes*. Agatha, Mary and Downing in *The Family Reunion*; Sir Henry Harcourt Reilly, Julia and Alex in *The Cocktail Party*, Eggerson in *The Confidential Clerk* and the loving Monica in *The Elder Statesman* are such characters who perform the choric function. Besides being the mouthpiece of the dramatist, these characters provide a running commentary and also play the role of *Helpers* in guiding the *Blinds* towards purgation and self-realization playing the role of auxiliary chorus in the plays of Eliot.

Then we also have certain speeches by characters depicting the inner permutations and the psychological conflict of their mind. They at times take the form of Hamlet-like soliloquies as in the case of Lord Claverton. Thus it may be safely concluded that in the later plays of Eliot, the chorus though not physically present on the stage, definitely stands in the wings. At times it even comes on the stage with a mask on.

Last but not least, a student of T.S. Eliot's plays can hardly overlook the quality of great poetry embedded in the chorus. The poetry is interfused with thought, language and feeling in such a manner as to produce real great poetry. The superb skill with which Eliot weaves the pattern of images to differentiate the levels of meaning an experience in his plays makes them a powerful instrument of communication. As Stephen Spender says, "After *The Family Reunion* he reduced what he called the 'dosage' of poetry in his later plays."[34]

But Eliot has all along felt that in a genuine drama the poetic and the dramatic elements have to be organically fused together. So the dramatic speech must be nearer the audience and the verse must be natural and elastic. It should also be poetic, dramatic and musical. It should have the ring of a living voice. In doing so he brings poetry into the world in which the audience lives.

Eliot as an artist has always been conscious of his obligations to the society. So as a dynamic member of the society with a powerful zeal for communication, he could visualize with acute sensibility the various uses to which poetry could be put to. Through poetry he could enjoy the prestige of a music hall comedian and could commemorate a public occasion. He could also celebrate a festival or a religious rite. He could even successfully amuse a crowd. He could do all this and much more. His poetry being essentially dramatic, he illustrates a progressive understanding of the dramatic structure and so Eliot's plays offer a living example of the integration of poetry into drama into the living theatre.

Thus we find that while writing his plays, Eliot was making a continual search for the right form and so all his poetic plays are experiments and no play in a repetition of what has gone before. As E. Martin Browne says, "Eliot was always determined to go on growing."[35] Eliot himself confirms this when he says:

"I have before my eyes a kind of mirage of the perfection of verse drama, which would be a design of human actions and of words, such as to present at once the two aspects of dramatic and of musical order.... To go far in this direction as it is possible to go, without losing that contact with the ordinary everyday world with which drama must come to terms, seems to me the proper aim of dramatic poetry."[36]

In this respect, "Eliot's endeavour to create a new genre which would be both dramatically compelling and spiritually profound in terms meaningful to the modern age is a goal which must be endorsed, especially when it has been espoused by one the major poetic talents of the twentieth century."[37]

To conclude, however, we may sum up our impression of T.S. Eliot's dramatic works and his use of the chorus, in the words of John Gross, "What Eliot has left is an example of unwavering artistic integrity, and a glimpse of what might be achieved: enough to persuade any successor that the undertaking is worthwhile."[38]

NOTES AND REFERENCES

1. Sharma, H.L. 1976. *T.S. Eliot—His Dramatic Theories*. New Delhi: S. Chand & Co. 75.
2. Bowra, C.M. 1959. *Primitive Song*. London: Oxford University Press. 32.
3. Vaughan. 2004. *Types of Tragic Drama*. Indian Reprint. Meerut: Shalabh Publishing House. 24-25.
4. Aristotle. *Poetics*. VI.
5. Lucas, F.L. 2003. *Tragedy*. London: Hoggarth Press. Indian Reprint. New Delhi: A.I.T.B.S. Publishers and Distributors. 82.
6. *Ibid.* 80.
7. Haigh, A.E. 1938. *The Tragic Drama of the Greeks*. Oxford: Clarendon Press. 152.

8. Lucas, F.L. 2003. *Tragedy*. London: Hoggarth Press. Indian Reprint. New Delhi: A.I.T.B.S. Publishers and Distributors. 82.
9. *Ibid*. 84-85.
10. Craig, Hardin. 1960. *English Religious Drama of the Middle Ages*. London: Oxford University Press. 1.
11. Lucas, F.L. 2003. *Tragedy*. London: Hoggarth Press. Indian Reprint. New Delhi: A.I.T.B.S. Publishers and Distributors. 86.
12. *Ibid*. 88-89.
13. Vaughan. 2004. *Types of Tragic Drama*. Indian Reprint. Meerut: Shalabh Publishing House. 223.
14. Eliot, T.S. 1936. *The Need for Poetic Drama, The Listener* (25th November, 1936). 955.
15. Eliot, T.S. 1969. *The Complete Poems and Plays of T.S. Eliot*. London: Faber and Faber. 122-23.
16. *Ibid*. 126.
17. *Ibid*.
18. *Ibid*.
19. Gioegio, Thechiori. 1959. *Tight Rope Walkers*. London: Routledge & Kegan Paul. 121.
20. Mathiessen, F.O. 1959. *The Achievement of T.S. Eliot*. New York: Oxford University Press. 162.
21. Kenner, Hugh. 1962. *Twentieth Century Views on T.S. Eliot* (John Peter: *Murder in the Cathedral*). N.J.: Prentice Hall Inc.159-160.
22. Gardner, Helen. 1949. *The Art of T.S. Eliot*. London: The Cresset Press. 136.
23. Jones, D.E. 1960. *The Plays of T.S. Eliot*. London: Routledge & Kegan Paul. 58.
24. Raymond, Williams. 1968. *Drama from Ibson to Eliot*. London: Chatto & Windus. 228.
25. Jones, D.E. 1960. *The Plays of T.S. Eliot*. London: Routledge & Kegan Paul. 59.
26. Eliot, T.S. 1958 (Poetry and Drama). *On Poetry and Poets*. London: Faber and Faber. 81.
27. Mathiessen, F.O. 1959. *The Achievement of T.S. Eliot*. New York: Oxford University Press. 166.
28. Eliot, T.S. 1969. *The Complete Poems and Plays of T.S. Eliot*. London: Faber and Faber. 301.
29. Jones, D.E. 1960. *The Plays of T.S. Eliot*. London: Routledge & Kegan Paul. 118.

30. Lumley, Frederick. 1956. *Trends in Twentieth Century Drama*. London: Rockliff. Quoted in Sharma, H.L. 1976. *T.S. Eliot—His Dramatic Theories*. New Delhi: S. Chand & Co. 80.
31. Eliot, T.S. 1964. *The Use of Poetry and the Use of Criticism*. London: Faber and Faber. 104.
32. Jones, D.E. 1960. *The Plays of T.S. Eliot*. London: Routledge & Kegan Paul. 104.
33. Bradbrook, M.C. 1965. *English Dramatic Form—A History of its Devclopment*. London: Chatto & Windus. 174.
34. Spender, Stephen. 1975. *Eliot*. Glassgow. Fontana/Collins. 211.
35. Singh, Parwati. 1988. *Character and Symbol in the Plays of T.S. Eliot*. Delhi: Capital Publishing House. 158.
36. Eliot, T.S. 1958 (Poetry and Drama). *On Poetry and Poets*. London: Faber and Faber Limited. 87.
37. Smith, Carol H. 1963. *T.S. Eliot's Dramatic Theory and Practice*. London: Oxford University Press. 239.
38. Gross, John. 1965. *Eliot from Ritual to Realism* in *Encounter*, Vol. XXIV, No. 3. 50. Quoted in Subhas Sarkar, 2006. *T.S. Eliot—The Dramatist*. New Delhi: Atlantic Publishers & Distributors (P) Ltd. 290.

Chronology

CHRONOLOGY OF THE LIFE AND CAREER OF T.S. ELIOT

1888   T.S. Eliot born in St. Louis, Missouri.

1906-09   Undergraduate at Harvard. Discovery of the Symbolists and Laforgue.

1909-10   Graduate student at Harvard. Early poems, including 'Portrait of a Lady' and beginnings of *Prufrock*.

1910-11   Studies in France and Germany. *Prufrock* completed.

1911-14   Graduate student at Harvard. Commenced work on the Philosophy of Francis Herbert Bradley.

1914-15   Study in Germany cut off by war. Residence at Oxford. Short satiric poems. *Prufrock* published in Chicago, June 1915.

               Marriage to Vivien Haigh-Wood, July 1915.

1915-16   Teaching and book reviewing London. Bradley thesis completed.

1917-20   Employee of Lloyd's Bank. Numerous editorial and reviewing assignments. Writing of French poems, quartrain poems, 'Gerontion' *Prufrock and Other Observations* published June, 1917. *Poems* published 1920. *The Sacred Wood*, 1920.

1921-25   London correspondent for *The Dial* (1921-22) and *La Nouvelle Revue Francaise* (1922-23). Editorship of *The Criterion* commenced October 1922. Dial Award for *The Waste Land*, 1922. *Poems 1909-1925*, including *The Hollow Men*. Joined Faber & Gwyer, later Faber & Faber, publishers.

1926-27	'Fragment of a Prologue,' 'Fragment of an Agon,' essays on Seneca.
1927-31	Confirmation in the Church of England and assumption of British citizenship, 1927. *Ariel Poems,* 1927-30; *Ash-Wednesday,* 1930; Essay on Dante, 1929; *Coriolan,* 1931.
1932	*Selected Essays,* including most of *The Sacred Wood.*
1932-34	*The Use of Poetry and the Use of Criticism* (1933), *After Strange Gods* (1934), *The Rock,* 1934.
1935	*Murder in the Cathedral, Poems, 1909–1935,* including 'Burnt Norton.'
1939	*The Family Reunion.*
1940-42	Appearance of 'East Coker,' 'The Dry Salvage,' and 'Little Gidding,' published with 'Burnt Norton' as *Four Quartets,* 1943.
1947	Death of T.S. Eliot's first wife, after long illness.
1948	Nobel Prize for Literature. *Notes Towards the Definition of Culture.*
1950	*The Cocktail Party.*
1955	*The Confidential Clerk.*
1957	Marriage to Valerie Fletcher, *On Poetry and Poets.*
1959	*The Elder Statesman.*
1964	T.S. Eliot dies.

Bibliography

Aristotle. 1987. *The Poetics*. Edited by S.H. Butcher. Indian Reprint. New Delhi: Kalyani Publishers.

Arnold, Matthew. *Merope*.

Bentley, Eric. 1964. *The Playwright as Thinker*. New York: Reynal and Hitchock.

Bowra, C.M. 1959. *Primitive Song*. London: Oxford University Press.

Bradbrook, M.C. 1965. *English Dramatic Form—A History of its Development*. London: Chatto & Windus.

Bradbrook, M.C. 1951. *T.S. Eliot*. A British Council Pamphlet. London: Longmans Green and Co.

Braybrook, Neville (Ed). 1958. *T.S. Eliot—A Symposium for His Seventieth Birthday*. London: Rupert Hart Davis.

Brooks, Cleanth. 1955. *Tragic Themes in Western Literature*. New Haven: Yale University Press.

Chambers, E.K. *The Medieval Stage*.

Chaturvedi, B.N. 1967. *English Poetic Drama of the Twentieth Century*. Gwalior: Kitab Ghar.

Coghill, Nevill (Ed.). 1963. *T.S. Eliot's The Family Reunion*. Delhi: Oxford University Press.

Coghill, Nevill (Ed). 1963. *T.S. Eliot's Murder in the Cathedral*. Delhi: Oxford University Press.

Cornford, Francis M. 1914. *The Origin of Attic Comedy*. London: Edwin Arnold.

Craig, Hardin. 1960. *English Religious Drama of the Middle Ages*. London: Oxford University Press.

Diaches, David. 1958. *The Present Age*. London: The Crescent Press.

Bibliography

Donnough, Dennis. 1959. *The Third Voice.* Princeton University Press.

Everyman's Encyclopaedia. 4th Edition, Vol. III.

Eliot, T.S. 1957. *On Poetry and Poets.* London: Faber and Faber.

Eliot, T.S. 1950. *Poetry and Drama.* The Theodore Spencer Memorial Lecture, Harvard University, Nov. 21, 1950. London: Faber and Faber.

Eliot, T.S. 1951. *Selected Essays.* London: Faber and Faber.

Eliot, T.S. 1936. *The Listener. November 25.*

Eliot, T.S. 1969. *The Complete Poems and Plays of T.S. Eliot.* London: Faber and Faber.

Eliot, T.S. 1936. "The Need for Poetic Drama." *The Listener,* November 25.

Eliot, T.S. 1949. *The Aims of Poetic Drama,* Presidential Address, The Poets' Theatre Guild.

Eliot, T.S. 1964. *The Sacred Wood.* London: Metheun & Co.

Eliot, T.S. 1953. *The Three Voices of Poetry.* Cambridge University Press.

Eliot, T.S. 1964. *The Use of Poetry and the Use of Criticism.* London: Faber and Faber.

Ellis-Fermo, Una. 1964. *The Frontiers of Drama.* London: Methuen & Co. Ltd.

Gardner, Helen. 1949. *The Art of T.S. Eliot.* London: The Cresset Press.

Gasner, John. *Masters of Drama.* 3rd revised edition and enlarged, Dover Publications Incorporated.

Gilbert Murray, *The Complete Plays of Aeschylus.* Introduction.

Gioegio, Thechiori. 1959. *Tight Rope Walkers.* London: Routledge & Kegan Paul.

Gowda, Anniah. 1972. *The Revival of English Poetic Drama.* New Delhi: Orient Longman.

Granville-Barker, H. 1937. *On Poetry and Drama. The Romances Lecture.* London: Sidwick & Jackson.

Gross, John. 1965. *Eliot from Ritual to Realism*, in *Encounter*, Vik, XXIV, No. 3, March, 1965. Quoted in Subhas Sarkar. 2006. *T.S. Eliot—The Dramatist*. New Delhi: Atlantic Publishers & Distributors (P) Ltd.

Haigh, A.E. 1938. *The Tragic Drama of the Greeks*. Oxford: Clarendon Press.

Harvey, Sir Paul. *Oxford Companion to Classical Literature*.

Headlam, Walter. 1907. *A Book of Greek Verse*. XVII.

Henn, T.R. 1956. *The Harvest of Tragedy*. London: Methuen & Co. Ltd.

Jones, D.E. 1960. *The Plays of T.S. Eliot*. London: Routledge & Kegan Paul.

Kenner, Hugh. 1962. *Twentieth Century Views: T.S. Eliot*. New Jersey: Prentice Hall.

Kenner, Hugh. 1966. *The Invisible Poet: T.S. Eliot*. University Paperbacks. London: Metheun & Co. Ltd.

Lever, Katherine. 1956. *The Art of Greek Comedy*. London: Metheun & Co. Ltd.

Lucas, F.L. 2003. *Tragedy*. London: Hoggarth Press. Indian Reprint. New Delhi: A.I.T.B.S. Publishers and Distributors.

Lumley, Fredrick. 1956. *New Trends in Twentieth Century Drama*. London: Rockliff.

Mathiessen, F.O. 1959. *The Achievement of T.S. Eliot*. New York: Oxford University Press.

Melchiori, Giorgio. 1959. *The Tightrope Walkers*. London: Routledge & Kegan Paul.

Methuen's Study-Aid. 1971. *Notes on T.S. Eliot's Murder in the Cathedral*. London: Methuen & Co. Ltd.

Michael Herbert. 2001. *York Notes on Selected Poems of T.S. Eliot*. London: York Press, First Indian Reprint.

Milton, John. *Samson Agonistes*.

Milton, John. *Paradise Lost*.

Nicoll, Allardyce. 1958. *British Drama*. London: George G. Harrap and Co. Ltd.

Nicoll, A. 1957. *Theory of Drama*. London: George G. Harrap & Co.

Nicoll, Allardyce. 1962. *The Theatre and Dramatic Theory*. London: George G. Harrap & Co.

P. Toyanbee and L. Whibley (Ed.). 1935. *Correspondence*.

Peacock, Ronald. 1957. *The Art of Drama*. London: Routledge & Kegan Paul.

Peacock, Reynold. 1946. *The Poet in the Theatre*. London: Routledge & Kegan Paul.

Roy, V.K. 1979. *T.S. Eliot: Quest for Belief*. Delhi: Ajanta Publications.

Seaars Jayne. 1955. *Mr. Eliot's Agon (Philological Quarterly, XXXIV)*.

Shakespeare. *Complete Works*.

Sharma, Jitendra Kumar. 1985. *Time & T.S. Eliot*. New Delhi: Sterling Publishers Private Limited.

Sharma, H.L. 1976. *T.S. Eliot—His Dramatic Theories*. New Delhi: S. Chand & Co.

Singh, Dr. Parwati. 1988. *Character and Symbol in the Plays of T.S. Eliot*. Delhi: Capital Publishing House.

Smith, Carol H. 1963. *T.S. Eliot's Dramatic Theory and Practice*. London: Oxford University Press.

Smith Kristian. 1961. *Poetry and Belief in the Works of T.S. Eliot*. London: Routledge & Kegan Paul.

Spender, Stephen. 1975. *Eliot*. Glassgow: Fontana/Collins.

Subhas Sarkar. 2006. *T.S. Eliot—The Dramatist*. New Delhi: Atlantic Publishers & Distributors (P) Ltd.

Thompson, George. 1941. *Aeschylus and Athens*. London: Oxford University Press.

Thouless, Priscilla. 1934. *Modern Poetic Drama*. Oxford: Basil Blackwell.

Titus, T.K. 2001. *A Critical Study of T.S. Eliot's Works*. New Delhi: Atlantic Publishers & Distributors (P) Ltd.

Varshney, R.L. (Ed.). *T.S. Eliot's Murder in the Cathedral*. Agra: Laxmi Narain Agrawal.

Vaughan. 2004. *Types of Tragic Drama*. Indian Reprint. Meerut: Shalabh Publishing House.

Williamson George. 1962. *A Reader's Guide to T.S. Eliot*. New York: The Noonday Press.

Raymond. Williams . 1954. *Drama from Ibson to Eliot*. Chatto & Windus.